Teaching
EVIDENCE-BASED WRITING:
Fiction

TEXTS AND LESSONS FOR SPOT-ON WRITING ABOUT READING

with **100** *Best-the-Test* **TIPS**

LESLIE BLAUMAN

http://resources.corwin.com/evidencebasedwriting-fiction

CL CORWIN LITERACY

T0354078

FOR INFORMATION:

Corwin
A SAGE Company
2455 Teller Road
Thousand Oaks, California 91320
(800) 233-9936
www.corwin.com

SAGE Publications Ltd.
1 Oliver's Yard
55 City Road
London EC1Y 1SP
United Kingdom

SAGE Publications India Pvt. Ltd.
B 1/I 1 Mohan Cooperative Industrial Area
Mathura Road, New Delhi 110 044
India

SAGE Publications Asia-Pacific Pte. Ltd.
3 Church Street
#10-04 Samsung Hub
Singapore 049483

Publisher: Lisa Luedeke
Editor: Wendy Murray
Editorial Development Manager: Julie Nemer
Editorial Assistant: Nicole Shade
Production Editor: Melanie Birdsall
Copy Editor: Sarah J. Duffy
Typesetter: C&M Digitals (P) Ltd.
Proofreader: Alison Syring
Cover and Interior Designer: Gail Buschman
Marketing Manager: Rebecca Eaton

Book, video, and mouse icons courtesy of iStock.

Printed in the United States of America

Library of Congress Cataloging-in-Publication Data

Names: Blauman, Leslie, author.

Title: Teaching evidence-based writing. Fiction : texts and lessons for spot-on writing about reading / Leslie Blauman.

Description: Thousand Oaks, California : Corwin, 2017. | Includes bibliographical references.

Identifiers: LCCN 2016025899 | ISBN 9781506360706 (pbk. : alk. paper)

Subjects: LCSH: Language arts (Elementary)—United States. | English language—Composition and exercises—Study and teaching (Elementary)—United States. | Composition (Language arts)—Study and teaching (Elementary)—United States. | Reading comprehension—Study and teaching (Elementary)—United States. | Critical thinking—Study and teaching (Elementary)—United States.

Classification: LCC LB1576 .B49827 2017 | DDC 372.6/044—dc23
LC record available at https://lccn.loc.gov/2016025899

This book is printed on acid-free paper.

16 17 18 19 20 10 9 8 7 6 5 4 3 2 1

CONTENTS

SECTION 1. *Evidence*   1

SECTION 2. *Relationships*   39

SECTION 3. *Themes* 83

SECTION 4. *Point of View* 107

Visit the companion website at
http://resources.corwin.com/evidencebasedwriting-fiction
for videos, write-about-reading templates, excerpts to write about,
and more downloadable resources.

VIDEO CLIPS

 Videos may also be accessed at the companion website, **http://resources.corwin.com/evidencebasedwriting-fiction**

Evidence

- **Video 1:** Students do the Excerpt to Write About activity with a short story

Relationships

- **Video 2:** Small-group novel discussions focused on character

Themes

- **Video 3:** A lesson on talking and writing about theme, using a popular novel

Point of View

- **Video 4:** A lesson on noticing and writing about point of view in a picture book

Visuals

- **Video 5:** Students read visuals for clues on mood, setting, and plot

Words and Structure

- **Video 6:** Attending to vocabulary and word choice in a text

WRITE-ABOUT-READING TEMPLATES

Evidence

Relationships

Themes

Point of View

Visuals

Words and Structure

EXCERPTS TO WRITE ABOUT

Evidence

Relationships

Themes

Point of View

Visuals

Words and Structure

DYNAMIC DUOS: ADDITIONAL IDEAS FOR TEACHING WITH THE TEXTS

Note: Every lesson in this book uses excerpts or whole pieces of amazing literature. These are the works my students love and that I lean on each year because there are so many aspects of reading you can explore with them. Here, I provide extra ideas for using these texts. Enjoy!

TEXT PAIR	LEADS AND ENDINGS	WORD CHOICE AND VOCABULARY	ELEMENTS OF LITERATURE	TEXT STRUCTURES
"Saturday at the Canal," "Dreams," and "Mother to Son"	Discuss the leads to these poems and the endings. How does each lead you into the poem? How do the endings leave the reader feeling?		Have students compare/contrast the themes in two of these poems. How does the speaker's point of view affect the theme?	
The Giver and *The Real Boy*		Consider the tone set in each piece. How does the author do it?	Compare/contrast how the author depicts the setting. How does setting impact the main characters and the plot?	
"The Circuit" *From The Circuit: Stories From the Life of a Migrant Child*, "The Julian Chapter" From *Auggie and Me: Three Wonder Stories*, and *The Promise*			How does the character define the plot? How does the character change in each of these stories due to another character's influence?	Think of character change. All three books are told from the first person point of view. How does the narrator affect reader understanding? How do illustrations depict character change?

TEXT PAIR	LEADS AND ENDINGS	WORD CHOICE AND VOCABULARY	ELEMENTS OF LITERATURE	TEXT STRUCTURES
Fish in a Tree and *The Tiger Rising*	The beginning of each of these books introduces us to the main character and causes the reader to infer. How do the authors do this? How does the ending of each excerpt answer questions asked at the beginning?	What types of figurative language are used in these books? How does this impact character development (and reader understanding of the main characters), plot, and theme?		
Here Where the Sunbeams Are Green and *Wonder*		Notice the author's word choice, especially choices that create voice. How does this enhance understanding of character?		Compare/contrast the text structure/ organization and how this impacts understanding of character and plot.
"My First Step to the White House" and "Mr. Nobody"	Compare/contrast the lead to each of these texts. How does the narrator/ speaker catch the reader's attention? How does the title match the story?			Compare/contrast text structure and how that depicts character response to problems.
"Eleven" and *No Two Snowflakes*		Compare/contrast how the author uses word choice to show character, plot, and setting.		Discuss how text structure influences reader understanding, especially inferences.

To Scott Haney.

Thanks for taking the writing journey with me.
You've been there every step of the way. My muse.

ACKNOWLEDGMENTS

A huge hug and thank you to my editor and friend, Wendy Murray. You are an inspiration. We started with a great idea, but you grew it and used your wisdom and vision to bring this book to life. You have this innate ability to envision and design beautiful books.

Thank you to my students—all 33 years' worth. Each year there is a magic. I learn right along with you, and I continue to be amazed by you each day.

A heartfelt thank you to the teachers with whom I work, here in Denver and across the country. I admire what you bring to your classrooms, and the way you change lives, even when faced with daunting challenges.

Thank you to Kate Blanchard for providing feedback on the lessons and layout. Besides being a dear friend, you are a talented educator, and your students are lucky to have you.

To the schools that opened their doors and classrooms to our film crew, many, many thanks! At Aspen Crossing—principal Scott Schleich, Jill Jesch and her third graders, and Kate Blanchard and Chad Blood and their fifth graders—your students are brilliant! At West Middle School—principal Kate Bergles, Carol Meyer and her fabulous sixth graders, and Kathryn Strickland and her tremendous eighth graders—the depth of the thinking blew me away! And finally to my fourth-grade students. Basically, "you rock!"

A shout-out to the film crew who did the video: David Stewart, Patrick Gillespie, Brandon Reich-Sweet, and Maya Ferrario. It was a blast! A huge thank you to video producer Julie Slattery for directing and keeping us on track.

Thank you to my CHVE "family"—the phenomenal educators, students, and parents that make it such an outstanding school. A special thank you to Clay Borchert, Jessica Yoffe, and Sue Beman, who keep the laughter alive. And to our captain, Molly Drvenkar, for keeping the joy (and sanity) in teaching! You always have what's best for kids at the forefront.

Thank you to the Corwin "family" who work their magic and bring books to life. I could write pages of accolades to you all: Lisa Shaw, Lisa Luedeke, Wendy Murray, Rebecca Eaton, Gail Buschman, Melanie Birdsall, Julie Nemer, Nicole Shade, Sarah J. Duffy, and Alison Syring.

Thank you to my friends, who are patient with me while I'm "working on the writing." Friends that are worth their weight in gold. Trina and Sue, especially—thanks for keeping me balanced! I love you!

My family in Washington—a family of teachers. Andy, Jill, Allison, and Mark. I'm truly blessed to have you in my life. And finally, my kids. I am so incredibly proud of you. Carolynn and John, I love the people you are and I can't wait to see where life takes you. Thank you for your support, love, and encouragement.

INTRODUCTION

Every writer goes into drafting a book with an operating metaphor—at least I do! For this one, I kept envisioning myself long-distance running on this wooded path in Colorado, or working out at the gym. Why these images? Because if we want students to be at the top of their game when it comes to writing, they need to practice it—a lot. And if we want students to become especially good at writing in response to reading, we need to do specific strength training so their minds work in particular ways as they analyze texts.

How do we give students this practice so that students' working metaphor isn't an ox pulling a heavy cart or some image of dull labor?

The answer is: Make sure the literature you read and mull is appealing and engaging to them. Period. That's why I've built the lessons and student activities in this book around popular novels, myths, and poems that are easy to get your hands on and your minds around. Excerpts from Gary Soto, Kate DiCamillo, Ralph Fletcher, Gary Paulsen, Sandra Cisneros, Eve Bunting—to name a few. Learning to support ideas with evidence from a text takes time, so my attitude is, the literature we use has to be exemplary and well worth such close attention.

Why does evidence-based writing matter?

The lofty answer is: It's a kind of writing that will serve students well throughout their school careers and lives, because no matter what we do, being able to deliver a well-reasoned line of thinking is valued in the world.

The teacher answer is: Helping our students get good at evidence-based writing is the gift that keeps on giving, because it applies in every content area and boosts reading, thinking, speaking, and listening skills, too.

The not-so-secret-agenda answer is: Writing in response to texts is huge on the standardized tests.

I am passionately against test prep (and so is the research, which has shown it isn't a good use of instructional time). In this book I provide lessons and practice that stay true to authentic examinations of literature, but mark my word, these materials will prepare your students for high-stakes tests. My fourth graders have scored above the district and the national average for well over a decade. While testing is not their favorite activity, they want to "show what they know." I ask if they prefer worksheets or "real-world learning." Emphatically they say "give us the books and the writing." My response—knock it out of the ballpark. And they do. They have internalized the power of reading and writing authentically. How is that for bragging rights?

In my heart of hearts, I know that teaching students how to read and write *authentically* will transfer to testing situations. Ideally, then, you will use the texts and lessons as amped-up practice within a reading and workshop model. However, I realize not every teacher can or wants to "do" workshop, so I designed everything to work in any literacy setting.

THE LITERATURE SKILLS IN FOCUS

- Evidence
- Relationships
- Themes
- Point of view
- Visuals
- Words and structure

THE STANDARDS ALIGNED

As this book goes to press, the Common Core State Standards (CCSS) face some backlash but are still the standards used in most states. Therefore, the standards I outline below are drawn from the CCSS. If you teach in a state that uses different standards, it doesn't matter one bit, for as you will see below, the writing and reading skills involved are timeless.

Writing Standard 9 states that students will "draw evidence from literary or informational texts to support analysis, reflection, and research." This in essence is *writing about reading*. The reading standards that the lessons in this book focus on are the following:

- **Reading 1:** Read closely to determine what the text says explicitly and to make logical inferences from it; cite specific textual evidence when writing or speaking to support conclusions drawn from the text.

- **Reading 2:** Determine central ideas of themes of a text and analyze their development; summarize the key supporting details and ideas.

- **Reading 3:** Analyze how and why individuals, events, and ideas develop and interact over the course of a text.

- **Reading 4:** Interpret words and phrases as they are used in a text, including determining technical, connotative, and figurative meanings, and analyze how specific word choices shape meaning or tone.

- **Reading 5:** Analyze the structure of texts, including how specific sentences, paragraphs, and larger portions of the text (e.g., a section, chapter, scene, or stanza) relate to one another and the whole.

- **Reading 6:** Assess how point of view or purpose shapes the content and style of a text.

- **Reading 7:** Integrate and evaluate content presented in diverse formats and media,

including visually and quantitatively, as well as in words.

- **Reading 8:** Analyze how two or more texts address similar themes or topics to build knowledge or to compare the approaches the authors take.

Notice that there are eight standards here and six sections of the book. Writing about words and phrases is combined with structure of texts in one section. Comparing and contrasting works is embedded throughout the lessons, as it transfers across the reading standards.

THE EXPECTATIONS FOR GRADES 6–8

While the standards remain the same, the sophistication changes as students progress through the grades. Verbs change, too. In Grades 3–5 students are generally describing or explaining. As they move to Grades 6–8, students are expected to *analyze*. These lessons are easily adapted to Grades 6–8 simply by having students analyze how the author writes or how the text is presented. In addition, the even-numbered lessons are all more *advanced* follow-up to the preceding lesson. Teachers of Grades 6–8 might simply skip to these for their students. Specific lessons that focus on Grades 6–8 have asterisks next to them in the table of contents.

It's all about balance. I use that word a lot as I work with teachers. Best practice. And best practice means incorporating rich texts in our classrooms. There are a lot of rich texts in this book. Use them. Practice with them. Use the organizers, but then move away from them and let the kids take control. The lessons in this book are meant to be the foundation for a solid start on writing about reading. My hope is that you use them to create a framework for a love of reading and writing in your classroom.

HOW TO USE THE LESSONS, EXCERPTS, AND GRAB AND GO PAGES

Key terms are defined for easy understanding.

You post these prompts and make copies for students' notebooks. The goal is for students to work independently, and these prompts provide structure while also moving students to be metacognitive.

LESSON 1

Ask and Answer Questions

Textual Evidence: Not all evidence is created equal; students need to choose those pieces of evidence (words, phrases, passages, illustrations) that provide the best proof of what they are asserting about the text.

PROMPTS FOR ASKING AND ANSWERING QUESTIONS

- What happens in this story, play, or poem?
- How is the author pulling me into the story? Making me curious? Where is the energy/tension coming from?
- As I read, what are the why, when, how, who, where, and what questions that arise? How can I answer them?
- What inferences can I make and what specific details help me?
- When I reread, can I find details to answer questions that begin with Who, What, Where, When, Why, and How?
- When I reread, can I find details that support "bigger" thinking about theme or character motivation?

 Available for download at
http://resources.corwin.com/evidencebasedwriting-fiction

BEST THE TEST

Test questions are designed to have one right answer, despite the fact that authentic reader questions seldom do. While we want students exploring real questions, we need to familiarize them with the testing genre. Teach your students to:

- Read test questions carefully. Highlight key words.
- Ask yourself: Is the question asking for more than one example? Is it a multi-step question?
- Mark multiple-choice answers that are obviously wrong "OW" to visually rule them out.
- Recognize "distracter" answers designed to trip you up. (It's the answer that if you're not paying attention looks right; it might repeat a word from the end of the text.)
- Prior to testing, devote a lesson to analyzing released test questions. Have students work in groups and create two-column charts labeled "Our Questions" and "Test Maker Questions," and have them record what they notice about the different types.
- Limit test prep! Short doses over a period of time go a long way versus every day, all day.

2

This section explicitly states how the lessons address test-taking skills and provides ideas to introduce students to the genre of standardized tests.

This section explains what you need ahead of time—both the materials and the key points in texts.

This section offers a quick view to find more resources.

LESSON PREP

• Choose a book that lends itself to asking both literal and inferential questions. I use Chris Van Allsburg's *The Stranger* in this lesson. Familiarize yourself with the text and flag pages that lend themselves to asking questions (pp. 5, 7, 9, 15, 19, 21, 22, 23, 24, 25).

INTRODUCE IT

1. Distribute prompts to students and/or display them on a wall as an anchor chart.

2. Also create your own anchor chart with the prompts.

3. Create a second anchor chart labeled with "Purpose: Asking Questions" and the book title.

4. Ask students to open their reading journals to record their thinking.

5. Write "Before" on the chart and tell students that readers ask questions before reading, even if it's just nanosecond wonderings about the title. Show the book cover and model and jot some of your questions. Have students copy the chart and write "Before" and jot at least three questions of their own.

6. Have students turn and talk. Add a few of their questions to the chart.

7. Now write "During" on the chart and tell students that readers ask questions as their thinking is evolving while they read.

8. Read aloud *The Stranger* or whichever text you are using, stopping at flagged pages. Model your questions, jotting them on the chart, and then turn over the work to students. That is, each time you pause in your read-aloud at a spot you've flagged, they are to jot a question and then share it with a partner.

9. Remind students to pay attention to the pictures when applicable. (Pages 22 and 24 of *The Stranger* have great question-provoking pictures.)

10. When you finish the book, write "After" on the chart. What questions do you still have? (Who was the Stranger?) Have students write an answer on their paper and discuss. (Students often answer "Jack Frost" or something similar.)

11. Go back to the text a second time (this could be on another day). Look at the questions students posed and have them find details that help to answer that question.

12. After revisiting, discuss new thinking and how asking questions led students to their answer.

13. Revisit the questions a third time—coding them L for answered *literally*, I for answered *inferentially*, and NA for *not answered* on the anchor chart. Have students code their own questions.

14. Write about reading: Co-construct a response to "Who was the Stranger?" using questions and evidence from the text so students get a feel for how this work helps one write a well-supported, well-reasoned response to text.

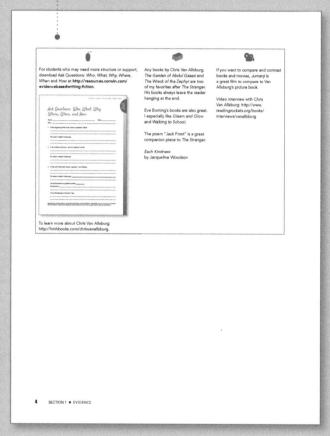

For students who may need more structure or support, download Ask Questions: *Who, What, Why, Where, When and How* at **http://resources.corwin.com/evidencebasedwriting-fiction**.

To learn more about Chris Van Allsburg: http://hmhbooks.com/chrisvanallsburg.

Any books by Chris Van Allsburg. *The Garden of Abdul Gasazi* and *The Wreck of the Zephyr* are two of my favorites after *The Stranger*. His books always leave the reader hanging at the end.

Eve Bunting's books are also great. I especially like *Gleam and Glow* and *Walking to School*.

The poem "Jack Frost" is a great companion piece to *The Stranger*.

Each Kindness by Jacqueline Woodson

If you want to compare and contrast books and movies, *Jumanji* is a great film to compare to Van Allsburg's picture book.

Video interview with Chris Van Allsburg: http://www.readingrockets.org/books/interviews/vanallsburg

Here is a short plan to follow, which begins with guided practice, includes student collaboration, and involves literature pieces in the book or readily available elsewhere. This section always incorporates a "Write About Reading" section.

Each lesson includes two Grab and Go reproducibles to share with students. One is a mentor text for students to annotate and write about, and the second is a Write-About-Reading template or task to provide additional writing. This "How To" page offers specific instructions on executing and extending the student practice.

HOW TO USE THE GRAB AND GO PAGES

- Distribute to students copies of Back Up Your Thinking on page 19 and the Gary Soto poem on page 20.

- Either in small groups, with a partner, or independently, students read and annotate the poem, using the same process you just modeled.

- Next, provide a focus question for students *or* allow them to pose their own question and record it in the center of the Back Up Your Thinking template.

- Students record their thinking on sticky notes as they reread the poem.

- Next, they use these notes to complete the Back Up Your Thinking template.

- Finally, students write a short response. (They can use the co-constructed response you did as a model.)

- **On another day**: Students can select a poem or a short text and use the same process to practice citing evidence and writing about it.

- **Ongoing**: You can reuse this excerpt and write-about-reading template for other purposes and in any of the lessons in this book.

SAMPLE TO SHARE WITH STUDENTS

What is the relationship between Liz and her father?

Liz didn't know her father very well since at the beginning of the book Liz is in the car and it says, "I sit shyly in the front seat of the car next to the stranger who is my father, my legs pulled up under the too-large wool shirt I am wearing. I practice his name to myself, whispering it under my breath. Daddy. Daddy. Saying it feels new. The war has lasted so long. He has been gone so long. Finally I look over at him timidly and speak aloud. 'Daddy,' I say, 'I've never gone hunting before. What if I don't know what to do?' 'Well, Liz,' he says, 'I've been thinking about that, and I've decided to put you in charge of the crow call. Have you ever operated a crow call?" They talk more as they ride, but it's obvious that her father has a sense of humor because he winks at Liz when the waitress at the diner thinks she's a boy because of the oversized shirt her father bought. He asks what's her favorite food and orders the cherry pie for her for breakfast. At this point you can see that they are getting to know each other. They continue to laugh together as they drive. Liz is "uneasy" with her father being a hunter--she's not used to it-as they walk through the woods. When she says, "Daddy,' I ask shyly, 'were you scared in the war?" it leads to a good conversation between them . . . At the end they are becoming dad and daughter because the story ends with "Then I put it into the pocket of my shirt and reach over out of my enormous cuff, and take my father's hand.'

There are completed classroom samples to share with your students as benchmarks.

Students learn by doing, so these Write-About-Reading templates scaffold their collaborative and independent work as they reread and interpret texts. These pages can also be used in other lessons in this book, or you can tweak them to fit your instructional needs.

GRAB & GO

Ask Questions

Name: _____ Date: _____

Title: _____

Directions:

- Record your questions on this page as you read through your independent reading book.
- When you finish, revisit the book and your questions and think about how your thinking changed as you read.
- Tie it all together by writing about how your thinking changed.

Questions before reading:

_____
_____
_____

Questions during reading:

_____
_____
_____

Questions after reading:

_____
_____
_____

How my thinking has changed, and why:

_____
_____
_____

This book includes 25 excerpts or complete pieces by top authors. You can use them for multiple purposes in this book's lessons and beyond.

EXCERPTS TO WRITE ABOUT

Number the Stars

by Lois Lowry

▶ In Chapter 1, titled "Why Are You Running?" we meet Annemarie, her little sister Kirsti, and Annemarie's friend Ellen as they are racing home from school in Copenhagen. They are stopped by a soldier who speaks German and asks them why they were running. After asking the girls other questions and inspecting their schoolbags, the soldiers allow them to go home, cautioning the girls not to run.

▶ As you read this, think about what questions you have and *why*. Write your questions in the margin. For example, why are the soldiers simply part of the landscape to Kirsti, but scarier for the other girls?

[pp. 5–6]

When they were almost home, Ellen whispered suddenly, "I was so scared."

"Me too," Annemarie whispered back.

As they turned to enter their building, both girls looked straight ahead, toward the door. They did it purposely so that they would not catch the eyes or the attention of two more soldiers, who stood with their guns on this corner as well. Kirsti scurried ahead of them through the door, chattering about the picture she was bringing home from kindergarten to show Mama. For Kirsti, the soldiers were simply part of the landscape, something that had always been there, on every corner, as unimportant as lampposts, throughout her remembered life.

"Are you going to tell your mother?" Ellen asked Annemarie as they trudged together up the stairs. "I'm not. My mother would be upset."

"No, I won't either. Mama would probably scold me for running on the street."

▶ Think about the question you asked. What in the text helped you ask that? Highlight the words, lines, or sentences. Think about your question. Is it about character, setting, the problem, or something else?

▶ But it was too late—Kirsti had already told their mother about the incident. This time notice the questions the characters ask. Jot your thinking about why these are important in the margins.

[pp. 6–7]

"Annemarie, what happened? What is Kirsti talking about?" her mother asked anxiously.

"Where's Ellen?" Mrs. Rosen had a frightened look.

"Ellen's in your apartment. She didn't realize you were here," Annemarie explained. "Don't worry. It wasn't anything. It was the two soldiers who stand on the corner of Osterbrogade—you've seen them; you know the tall one with the long neck, the one who looks like a silly giraffe?" She told her mother and Mrs. Rosen of the incident, trying to make it sound humorous and unimportant. But their uneasy looks didn't change.

(Continued)

SECTION 1

Evidence

Reading is thinking! It's an amazing exchange between the mind of the reader and the mind of the author. In this section, I share lessons and student practice that reveal just how this transaction works.

As students read, their part of the deal is to ask questions, use their knowledge, use the author's sensory details to envision, be attentive to moments when the author expects us to infer, and so on. The author's part of the deal was writing a text that is clear and that in essence uses thousands of details to create a well-ordered whole. This is where the importance of a reader "finding evidence" comes into play, because the reader has to "grab and go" with the *most important* details. We do the same thing when we sort through any body of information in our lives, from a political speech to a medical report. So this "weighing the facts" is not just a school or test skill—it's a life skill.

In literature, a reader notices the details that count most in a text, synthesizing them to arrive at theories about a character or theme. Then, when reflecting on a text—or writing about it during an exam—the reader uses these details to support her interpretation. You think Katniss is a loyal, compassionate person? Prove it. You think the turning point for Auggie in *Wonder* occurs at the end of Chapter 4? Show me where the author is telling you that.

But let's back up a minute: Answering these questions with details from the text begins with the reader *asking* questions! Students must ask questions about character, plot, theme, point of view, vocabulary, and so on. In the lessons that follow, your students will learn how to be super-curious readers and practice summarizing, a skill essential to solidifying and stating one's comprehension (Fisher, Frey, & Hattie, 2016).

Watch Leslie Teach!

Video 1: **Watch Leslie use the Excerpt to Write About activity to help students find evidence by asking questions.**

Go to **http://resources.corwin.com/evidencebasedwriting-fiction** to see the lessons and guided practice in action.

To read a QR code, you must have a smartphone or tablet with a camera. We recommend that you download a QR code reader app that is made specifically for your phone or tablet brand.

Ask and Answer Questions

Textual Evidence: Not all evidence is created equal; students need to choose those pieces of evidence (words, phrases, passages, illustrations) that provide the best proof of what they are asserting about the text.

PROMPTS FOR ASKING AND ANSWERING QUESTIONS

- What happens in this story, play, or poem?

- How is the author pulling me into the story? Making me curious? Where is the energy/tension coming from?

- As I read, what are the *why, when, how, who, where,* and *what* questions that arise? How can I answer them?

- What inferences can I make and what specific details help me?

- When I reread, can I find details to answer questions that begin with Who, What, Where, When, Why, and How?

- When I reread, can I find details that support "bigger" thinking about theme or character motivation?

 Available for download at
http://resources.corwin.com/evidencebasedwriting-fiction

BEST THE TEST

Test questions are designed to have one right answer, despite the fact that authentic reader questions seldom do. While we want students exploring real questions, we need to familiarize them with the testing genre. Teach your students to:

- Read test questions carefully. Highlight key words.

- Ask yourself: Is the question asking for more than one example? Is it a multi-step question?

- Mark multiple-choice answers that are obviously wrong "OW" to visually rule them out.

- Recognize "distracter" answers designed to trip you up. (It's the answer that if you're not paying attention looks right; it might repeat a word from the end of the text.)

- Prior to testing, devote a lesson to analyzing released test questions. Have students work in groups and create two-column charts labeled "Our Questions" and "Test Maker Questions," and have them record what they notice about the different types.

- Limit test prep! Short doses over a period of time go a long way versus every day, all day.

LESSON PREP

- Choose a book that lends itself to asking both literal and inferential questions. I use Chris Van Allsburg's *The Stranger* in this lesson. Familiarize yourself with the text and flag pages that lend themselves to asking questions (pp. 5, 7, 9, 15, 19, 21, 22, 23, 24, 25).

INTRODUCE IT

1. Distribute prompts to students and/or display them on a wall as an anchor chart.

2. Also create your own anchor chart with the prompts.

3. Create a second anchor chart labeled with "Purpose: Asking Questions" and the book title.

4. Ask students to open their reading journals to record their thinking.

5. Write "Before" on the chart and tell students that readers ask questions before reading, even if it's just nanosecond wonderings about the title. Show the book cover and model and jot some of your questions. Have students copy the chart and write "Before" and jot at least three questions of their own.

6. Have students turn and talk. Add a few of their questions to the chart.

7. Now write "During" on the chart and tell students that readers ask questions while they read as their thinking is evolving.

8. Read aloud *The Stranger* or whichever text you are using, stopping at flagged pages. Model your questions, jotting them on the chart, and then turn over the work to students. That is, each time you pause in your read-aloud at a spot you've flagged, they are to jot a question and then share it with a partner.

9. Remind students to pay attention to the pictures when applicable. (Pages 22 and 24 of *The Stranger* have great question-provoking pictures.)

10. When you finish the book, write "After" on the chart. What questions do you still have? (Who was the Stranger?) Have students write an answer on their paper and discuss. (Students often answer "Jack Frost" or something similar.)

11. Go back to the text a second time (this could be on another day). Look at the questions students posed and have them find details that help to answer that question.

12. After revisiting, discuss new thinking and how asking questions led students to their answer.

13. Revisit the questions a third time—coding them L for answered *literally*, I for answered *inferentially*, and NA for *not answered* on the anchor chart. Have students code their own questions.

14. **Write about reading:** Co-construct a response to "Who was the Stranger?" using questions and evidence from the text so students get a feel for how this work helps one write a well-supported, well-reasoned response to text.

For students who may need more structure or support, download Ask Questions: *Who, What, Why, Where, When* and *How* at **http://resources.corwin.com/ evidencebasedwriting-fiction**.

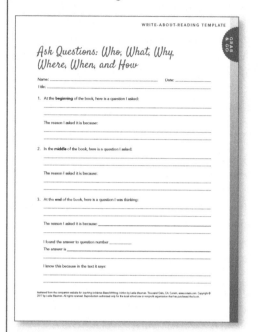

To learn more about Chris Van Allsburg: http://hmhbooks.com/chrisvanallsburg.

Any books by Chris Van Allsburg. *The Garden of Abdul Gasazi* and *The Wreck of the Zephyr* are two of my favorites after *The Stranger*. His books always leave the reader hanging at the end.

Eve Bunting's books are also great. I especially like *Gleam and Glow* and *Walking to School*.

The poem "Jack Frost" is a great companion piece to *The Stranger*.

Each Kindness by Jacqueline Woodson

If you want to compare and contrast books and movies, *Jumanji* is a great film to compare to Van Allsburg's picture book.

Video interview with Chris Van Allsburg: http://www. readingrockets.org/books/ interviews/vanallsburg

HOW TO USE THE GRAB AND GO PAGES

- Distribute to students copies of the Ask Questions template on page 6 and the short story "Eleven" by Sandra Cisneros on page 7.

- Tell students that as they read the story, they should jot questions they have before they read, during, and after they finish, using sticky notes or the margins.

- Reread the story excerpt, now having students notice new details and wonder different things. You can do this as a class if students need support or have students work collaboratively while you circulate, listening in. Students can share their thinking and try to answer one another's questions.

- Have students record their latest thinking on the Ask Questions template.

- **On another day**: Have students repeat this process with a picture book or short story you or they have chosen.

- **Ongoing**: You can adapt the Grab and Go Ask Questions template for many purposes! For example, you might have students pay attention only to plot, or main idea, or character. Or you might zero in on the question at the bottom of the organizer.

- Reuse this short story for *any* of the lessons in this book!

MORE TEMPLATES TO SHARE WITH STUDENTS

Reasons to Ask Questions

If you are curious about something

If you don't understand

If you want to predict something

If you wonder something

If you notice something

If you want to make something more clear

Questions That Make You Slow Down and Search

Questions that make you slow down and search, looking in more than one place for answers: What if? I wonder why? How come? Think of these questions as branches of a tree that stretch your thinking.

Why would?

What caused?

What are some examples of _____?

How are _____ and _____ similar?

How are _____ and _____ different?

Questions that are literal and right on the page!

Who?

What?

When?

Where?

How?

 Available for download at **http://resources.corwin.com/evidencebasedwriting-fiction**

GRAB & GO

Ask Questions

Name: _____ Date: _____

Title: _____

Directions:

- Record your questions on this page as you read through your independent reading book.
- When you finish, revisit the book and your questions and think about how your thinking changed as you read.
- Tie it all together by writing about how your thinking changed.

Questions before reading:

_____

_____

_____

Questions during reading:

_____

_____

_____

Questions after reading:

_____

_____

_____

How my thinking has changed, and why:

_____

_____

_____

Available for download at **http://resources.corwin.com/evidencebasedwriting-fiction**

"Eleven"

by Sandra Cisneros

What they don't understand about birthdays and what they never tell you is that when you're eleven, you're also ten, and nine, and eight, and seven, and six, and five, and four, and three, and two, and one. And when you wake up on your eleventh birthday you expect to feel eleven, but you don't. You open your eyes and everything's just like yesterday, only it's today. And you don't feel eleven at all. You feel like you're still ten. And you are—underneath the year that makes you eleven.

Like some days you might say something stupid, and that's the part of you that's still ten. Or maybe some days you might need to sit on your mama's lap because you're scared, and that's the part of you that's five. And maybe one day when you're all grown up maybe you will need to cry like if you're three, and that's okay. That's what I tell Mama when she's sad and needs to cry. Maybe she's feeling three.

Because the way you grow old is kind of like an onion or like the rings inside a tree trunk or like my little wooden dolls that fit one inside the other, each year inside the next one. That's how being eleven years old is.

You don't feel eleven. Not right away. It takes a few days, weeks even, sometimes even months before you say Eleven when they ask you. And you don't feel smart eleven, not until you're almost twelve. That's the way it is.

Only today I wish I didn't have only eleven years rattling inside me like pennies in a tin Band-Aid box. Today I wish I was one hundred and two instead of eleven because if I was one hundred and two I'd have known how to tell her it wasn't mine instead of just sitting there with that look on my face and nothing coming out of my mouth.

"Whose is this?" Mrs. Price says, and she holds the red sweater up in the air for all the class to see. "Whose? It's been sitting the coatroom for a month."

"Not mine," says everybody. "Not me."

"It has to belong to somebody," Mrs. Price keeps saying, but nobody can remember. It's an ugly sweater with red plastic buttons and a collar and sleeves all stretched out like you could use it for a jump rope. It's maybe a thousand years old and even if it belonged to me I wouldn't say so.

Maybe because I'm skinny, maybe because she doesn't like me, that stupid Sylvia Saldivar says, "I think it belongs to Rachel." An ugly sweater like that all raggedy and old, but Mrs. Price believes her. Mrs. Price takes the sweater and puts it right on my desk, but when I open my mouth nothing comes out.

"That's not, I don't, you're not. . . . Not mine," I finally say in a little voice that was maybe me when I was four.

"Of course it's yours," Mrs. Price says. "I remember you wearing it once." Because she's older and the teacher, she's right and I'm not.

Not mine, not mine, not mine, but Mrs. Price is already turning to page thirty-two, and math problem number four. I don't know why but all of a sudden I'm feeling sick inside, like the part of me that's three wants to come out of my eyes, only I squeeze them shut tight and bite down on my teeth real hard and try to remember today I am eleven, eleven. Mama is making a cake for me for tonight, and when Papa comes home everybody will sing Happy birthday, happy birthday to you.

But when the sick feeling goes away and I open my eyes, the red sweater's still sitting there like a big red mountain. I move the red sweater to the corner of my desk with my ruler. I move my pencil and books and eraser as far from it as possible. I even move my chair a little to the right. Not mine, not mine, not mine.

In my head I'm thinking how long till lunchtime, how long till I can take the red sweater and throw it over the schoolyard fence, or leave it hanging

(Continued)

(Continued)

on a parking meter, or bunch it up into a little ball and toss it in the alley. Except when math period ends Mrs. Price says loud and in front of everybody, "Now, Rachel, that's enough," because she sees I've shoved the red sweater to the tippy-tip corner of my desk and it's hanging all over the edge like a waterfall, but I don't care.

"Rachel," Mrs. Price says. She says it like she's getting mad. "You put that sweater on right now and no more nonsense."

"But it's not—"

"Now!" Mrs. Price says.

This is when I wish I wasn't eleven, because all the years inside of me—ten, nine, eight, seven, six, five, four, three, two and one—are pushing at the back of my eyes when I put one arm through one sleeve of the sweater that smells like cottage cheese, and then the other arm through the other and stand there with my arms apart like if the sweater hurts me and it does, all itchy and full of germs that aren't even mine.

That's when everything I've been holding in since this morning, since when Mrs. Price put the sweater on my desk, finally lets go, and all of a sudden I'm crying in front of everybody. I wish I was invisible but I'm not. I'm eleven and it's my birthday today and I'm crying like I'm three in

front of everybody. I put my head down on the desk and bury my face in my stupid clown-sweater arms. My face all hot and spit coming out of my mouth because I can't stop the little animal noises from coming out of me, until there aren't any more tears left in my eyes, and it's just my body shaking like when you have the hiccups, and my whole head hurts like when you drink milk too fast.

But the worst part is right before the bell rings for lunch. That stupid Phyllis Lopez, who is even dumber than Sylvia Saldivar, says she remembers the red sweater is hers! I take it off right away and give it to her, only Mrs. Price pretends like everything's okay.

Today I'm eleven. There's a cake Mama's making for tonight, and when Papa comes home from work we'll eat it. There'll be candles and presents and everybody will sing Happy birthday, happy birthday to you, Rachel, only it's too late.

I'm eleven today. I'm eleven, ten, nine, eight, seven, six, five, four, three, two and one, but I wish I was one hundred and two. I wish I was anything but eleven, because I want today to be far away already, far away like a runaway balloon, like a tiny o in the sky, so tiny-tiny you have to close your eyes to see it.

▶ **Notice all the similes. What might the author be trying to communicate about the girl's thoughts/emotions? Jot down some ideas.**

▶ **Read the lines aloud to yourself. What do you hear? Do the words sound calm or excited? Explain.**

Source: From *Woman Hollering Creek.* Copyright © 1991 by Sandra Cisneros. Published by Vintage Books, a division of Penguin Random House, Inc., New York, and originally in hardcover by Random House, Inc. By permission of Susan Bergholz Literary Services, New York, NY, and Lamy, NM. All rights reserved.

Note: This story by Sandra Cisneros is powerful in a hundred different ways! Students are highly engaged by it because of its relatable topic and themes (shame, how we carry younger selves inside us, justice). Notice the author's use of first person narration. (How completely different it would have been if written in the third person!) Cisneros captures the voice of an 11-year-old so well. Have students notice the way the story opens and closes with the attention to ages and how it adds to the meaning of the story and develops the character—and also enhances voice, and the cadence of the prose ("when you are eleven, you're also ten, and nine, and eight, and seven . . ."). Cisneros uses a parade of similes ("grow old is kind of like an onion or like the rings inside a tree trunk or like my little wooden dolls that fit one inside the other, each year inside the next one") to create an effect.

Use this story again and again to have students look at such elements as use of dialogue, words that are right-on for the character, secondary characters (like the mother) that deepen the theme. "Eleven" is also a powerful mentor text, as students are often inspired to write their own narratives using this story's basic structure.

Ask and Answer Questions Using Details

BEST THE TEST

Characters and their troubles are the heart of fiction, so test questions about them abound! Students can improve their test savvy by tuning in to characters' moments of upset. These "Why me?!" moments signal important character traits and maybe even character growth. They often come at a chapter's end, but not always, and may be a charged exchange with others or a time when the character is calm and alone. Help students recognize:

● When characters ask questions in the text, that is a signal for the reader to begin searching for an answer.

● In lessons and class discussions, guide students to notice the wishes, worries, and conflicts that simmer beneath a character's questions.

● "Do you trust him?" "So what are you going to do?" "Why is this happening?" "Whoa, what am I going to do now that I know this?" are all markers of a pivotal moment, when a main character is facing other people and events that compel him to either respond in the same old way or dare to do something surprising and new.

● Be Sherlock Holmes! Notice what the character *thinks and does* in these moments because this becomes the *evidence* to cite when asked to support reasoning on exams.

LESSON PREP

● Choose texts in which characters ask questions that drive the story by revealing either events, key conflicts, or theme.

● Photocopy the Lois Lowry novel excerpts (page 14) and the Ask Questions template (page 6) for each student.

INTRODUCE IT

1. Model asking questions with a shared text. Model how to notice and answer character's questions, too.

2. Guide students through the text and make it explicit how the questions a reader seeks answers to helps the reader to understand.

3. Use this and other excerpts to help students discover that asking questions is a part of sympathizing with characters, piecing things together as we seek to really understand their experience. Relate the question strategy to the concept of empathy: "You never really understand someone until you walk a mile in their shoes."

For English language learners (ELLs) and students who may need extra support, use the form Ask and Answer the Questions Characters Ask at **http://resources.corwin.com/evidencebased writing-fiction.**

Number the Stars by Lois Lowry

Crenshaw by Katherine Applegate

The One and Only Ivan by Katherine Applegate

Dug's Special Mission: https://youtu.be/9w6q07ARudw

Number the Stars movie trailer: https://youtu.be/B_i23_NuTpc

Background information on *Number the Stars:* http://teacherweb.com/NJ/TuckertonElementary School/MrHewitt/ns_history.pdf

HOW TO USE THE GRAB AND GO PAGES

- Distribute to students copies of Ask and Answer Questions on page 12 and the Lois Lowry novel excerpts on pages 14 and 15.

- Tell students that the quotes are from the first chapter of *Number the Stars* by Lois Lowry. Guide students to notice that Lowry does not provide background on the Nazis or World War II at the outset, but as a talented fiction writer she has the *characters* pose questions that are meant to nudge the reader to realize the setting and, ultimately, the problem.

- Ask students to read the excerpts and, in the margins, jot questions they have and predictions about the answers to the questions characters ask.

- Have students annotate *why* these might be important to the story.

- Have students discuss their thinking with peers.

OR

- Read *Number the Stars* as a class in its entirety, holding onto student-generated questions and important questions characters ask. Notice and discuss how thinking changes over the course of the book.

- **Ongoing:** Start a collection of excerpts or texts that you can turn to for modeling questions. Adapt the Ask and Answer Questions template (page 12) to focus on specific skills (discerning theme, point of view, characterization, plot, etc.).

- Have students write questions at the end of the chapter in books they are independently reading.

- Have students use sticky notes to record questions they have over the course of a text. Be ready to share and discuss these questions.

- Guide students to discuss their questions during group or book clubs.

TIPS FOR ANSWERING SHORT-ANSWER QUESTIONS

- Read the whole question carefully! Remember, some questions have more than one question.

- Think about what the question is asking and where in the passage you should look to find the information.

- Write your answer. Remember: Write in complete sentences. Lift lines from the question into your answer, but don't start with "because."

- Include evidence from the text to support your answer. Use "evidence terms" to show that proof.

- Reread the question. Did you answer *all of it*?

- Reread your answer. Does it make sense?

 Available for download at **http://resources.corwin.com/evidencebasedwriting-fiction**

Ask and Answer Questions

Name: _____ Date: _____

Title: _____

Directions:

- In the space below, write three (3) "thick" questions from your reading this week. What would be great questions to ask others who have read this section of the book?

- Write the answer to each of your questions. Make sure to include evidence from the text (lift a line!).

- Write one lingering question that you have that you think might be answered later in the text. Why is that important to you?

1. THICK question: _____

_____

_____

_____

_____

_____

Answer to the question: _____

_____

_____

_____

_____

_____

2. THICK question: _____

_____

_____

_____

_____

_____

(Continued)

(Continued)

Answer to the question: _____

_____

_____

_____

_____

_____

3. THICK question: _____

_____

_____

_____

_____

_____

Answer to the question: _____

_____

_____

_____

_____

_____

A lingering question that you have that can't be answered *yet:* _____

_____

_____

_____

_____

WHY you think it's important: _____

_____

_____

_____

_____

EXCERPTS TO WRITE ABOUT

Number the Stars

by Lois Lowry

▶ In Chapter 1, titled "Why Are You Running?" we meet Annemarie, her little sister Kirsti, and Annemarie's friend Ellen as they are racing home from school in Copenhagen. They are stopped by a soldier who speaks German and asks them why they were running. After asking the girls other questions and inspecting their schoolbags, the soldiers allow them to go home, cautioning the girls not to run.

▶ As you read this, think about what questions you have and *why*. Write your questions in the margin. For example, why are the soldiers simply part of the landscape to Kirsti, but scarier for the other girls?

> [pp. 5–6]
>
> When they were almost home, Ellen whispered suddenly, "I was so scared."
>
> "Me too," Annemarie whispered back.
>
> As they turned to enter their building, both girls looked straight ahead, toward the door. They did it purposely so that they would not catch the eyes or the attention of two more soldiers, who stood with their guns on this corner as well. Kirsti scurried ahead of them through the door, chattering about the picture she was bringing home from kindergarten to show Mama. For Kirsti, the soldiers were simply part of the landscape, something that had always been there, on every corner, as unimportant as lampposts, throughout her remembered life.
>
> "Are you going to tell your mother?" Ellen asked Annemarie as they trudged together up the stairs. "I'm not. My mother would be upset."
>
> "No, I won't either. Mama would probably scold me for running on the street."

▶ Think about the question you asked. What in the text helped you ask that? Highlight the words, lines, or sentences. Think about your question. Is it about character, setting, the problem, or something else?

▶ But it was too late—Kirsti had already told their mother about the incident. This time notice the questions the characters ask. Jot your thinking about why these are important in the margins.

> [pp. 6–7]
>
> "Annemarie, what happened? What is Kirsti talking about?" her mother asked anxiously.
>
> "Where's Ellen?" Mrs. Rosen had a frightened look.
>
> "Ellen's in your apartment. She didn't realize you were here," Annemarie explained. "Don't worry. It wasn't anything. It was the two soldiers who stand on the corner of Osterbrogade—you've seen them; you know the tall one with the long neck, the one who looks like a silly giraffe?" She told her mother and Mrs. Rosen of the incident, trying to make it sound humorous and unimportant. But their uneasy looks didn't change.

(Continued)

(Continued)

▶ **As you read the next section, what questions do you have? Do the capitalized words like *Resistance* and *Nazis* signal you to ask questions? Jot all your thinking in the margin. Think about how Annemarie's trying to figure things out draws you in.**

[pp. 7–8]

She spoke in a low voice to Ellen's mother. "They must be edgy because of the latest Resistance incidents. Did you read in *De Frie Danske* about the bombings in Hillerod and Norrebro?"

Although she pretended to be absorbed in unpacking her schoolbooks, Annemarie listened, and she knew what her mother was referring to. *De Frie Danske*—The Free Danes—was an illegal newspaper; Peter Neilsen brought it to them occasionally, carefully folded and hidden among ordinary books and papers, and Mama always burned it after she and Papa had read it. But Annemarie heard Mama and Papa talk, sometimes at night, about the news they received that way: news of sabotage against the Nazis, bombs hidden and exploded in the factories that produced war materials, and industrial railroad lines damaged so that the goods couldn't be transported.

And she knew what Resistance meant. Papa had explained, when she overheard the word and asked. The Resistance fighters were Danish people—no one knew who, because they were very secret—who were determined to bring harm to the Nazis however they could. They damaged the German trucks and cars, and bombed their factories. They were very brave. Sometimes they were caught and killed.

▶ **How do your questions help you understand the story? Do they make you want to read further to find out more? Why?**

▶ **After Mrs. Rosen leaves, the girls ask their mother if there is any food. There is bread, but no butter. As you read their dialogue and the end of the chapter, think about one big question that you're left with.**

[pp. 9–10]

Kirsti sighed as Annemarie went to the breadbox in the kitchen. "I wish I could have a cupcake," she said. "A big yellow cupcake, with pink frosting."

Her mother laughed. "For a little girl, you have a long memory," she told Kirsti. "There hasn't been any butter, or sugar for cupcakes, for a long time. A year, at least."

"When will there be cupcakes again?"

"When the war ends," Mrs. Johansen said. She glanced through the window, down to the street corner where the soldiers stood, their faces impassive beneath the metal helmets. "When the soldiers leave."

▶ **Look back through your questions. What do you notice about them?**

Note: As you and your students read the rest of Chapter 1, notice how in the dialogue on pages 9–10, Annemarie's younger sister, Kirsti, wishes for "a big yellow cupcake, with pink frosting" and asks, "When will there be cupcakes again?" This exchange beautifully sets up the ways in which the author uses this 5-year-old viewpoint to remind readers of both the evil of the Nazi regime and the strength of innocence and goodness.

Use Details and Examples

Cite Specific Textural Evidence: Students should be able to quote a specific passage from the text to support all claims, assertions, or arguments about what a text means or says. Evidence comes from within the text itself, not from the reader's opinion or experience.

Key Details: Parts of a text that support the main idea and enable the reader to draw conclusions and infer what the text or a portion of the text is about.

PROMPTS FOR USING DETAILS AND EXAMPLES

- What do I know/wonder about the author/book as I sit down to read?

- What are some ways I can recall and "hold" my thinking?

- Which specific details are most important?

- What would I quote to help explain the author's meaning?

- What does the author assume I know?

- What details/direct quotes can I point to that most support what I am inferring?

 Available for download at
http://resources.corwin.com/evidencebasedwriting-fiction

BEST THE TEST

Citing evidence, also called providing details, is a key test skill. Test takers are often asked to first select a response from multiple choices and then provide the detail that supports their thinking. Tips:

- "Drag and drop" questions and "identifying multiple details" show up often on tests, so periodically share examples of these tasks.

- Remember that citing evidence is an important component in opinion and argument writing, so you can get a lot of test practice under students' belts through writing.

LESSON PReP

- Choose a book that fits your purpose for citing details (character, plot, theme, etc.). Lois Lowry's memoir *Crow Call* is what I model here.

- Familiarize yourself with the text and have your main question or craft moments marked (e.g., pp. 4–6, "I sit shyly in the front seat of the car next to the stranger who is my father, my legs pulled up under the too-large wool shirt I am wearing. I practice his name to myself, whispering it under my breath. *Daddy. Daddy.* Saying it feels new. The war has lasted so long. He has been gone so long."). Your guiding question can be: Why is the title of the book *Crow Call*? Or what is the relationship between Liz and her father?

INTRODUCe IT

1. Distribute prompts to students and/or display them on a wall as anchor chart.

2. Also create your own anchor chart with the prompts.

3. Read aloud *Crow Call* (or whatever book you've chosen). Think aloud as you read, and record your question in the center. Mark your thinking and the evidence that supports the answer to your question on sticky notes. (Possible junctures are pp. 11, 13, 14, 16, 18, 22, 24, 26, 27.)

4. In this book an important page for discerning the relationship and ultimately the power of the crow call is on page 16 ("Daddy," I ask shyly, "were you scared in the war?"). This begins a sequence of dialogue that is important to both the plot and theme, along with their relationship. Pull out the importance of questions for citing evidence.

5. When you finish the book, read aloud your original question and have students discuss. Ask: How do you know this is true? How can we prove our answer?

6. Revisit the sticky notes and place them in the Evidence bubbles on the Back Up Your Thinking handout and record *how* they helped you know— *why* the evidence supports your thinking.

7. **Write about reading:** Co-construct a short response to the question. Write down the question. Answer the question. Cite the evidence (lift a line if necessary), and Explain how the evidence supports your thinking. This ACE acronym is a great way to structure writing for test prompts.

8. Tell students they will be using this same process as they practice asking questions about their reading and finding the evidence to support or "prove" their answers.

To learn more about Lois Lowry:

- http://loislowry.com

- http://www.biography.com/people/lois-lowry

The Lotus Seed by Sherry Garland

Video interview with Lois Lowry:
http://www.readingrockets.org/books/interviews/lowry

Crow Calls: https://youtu.be/xg92vEt4sW0

Crow Calling:
https://youtu.be/4UkvgEC8Qyc

HOW TO USE THE GRAB AND GO PAGES

- Distribute to students copies of Back Up Your Thinking on page 19 and the Gary Soto poem on page 20.

- Either in small groups, with a partner, or independently, students read and annotate the poem, using the same process you just modeled.

- Next, provide a focus question for students *or* allow them to pose their own question and record it in the center of the Back Up Your Thinking template.

- Students record their thinking on sticky notes as they reread the poem.

- Next, they use these notes to complete the Back Up Your Thinking template.

- Finally, students write a short response. (They can use the co-constructed response you did as a model.)

- **On another day**: Students can select a poem or a short text and use the same process to practice citing evidence and writing about it.

- **Ongoing:** You can reuse this excerpt and write-about-reading template for other purposes and in any of the lessons in this book.

SAMPLE TO SHARE WITH STUDENTS

What is the relationship between Liz and her father?

Liz didn't know her father very well since at the beginning of the book Liz is in the car and it says, "I sit shyly in the front seat of the car next to the stranger who is my father, my legs pulled up under the too-large wool shirt I am wearing. I practice his name to myself, whispering it under my breath. Daddy. Daddy. Saying it feels new. The war has lasted so long. He has been gone so long. Finally I look over at him timidly and speak aloud. 'Daddy,' I say, 'I've never gone hunting before. What if I don't know what to do?' 'Well, Liz,' he says, 'I've been thinking about that, and I've decided to put you in charge of the crow call. Have you ever operated a crow call?'" They talk more as they ride, but it's obvious that her father has a sense of humor because he winks at Liz when the waitress at the diner thinks she's a boy because of the oversized shirt her father bought. He asks what's her favorite food and orders the cherry pie for her for breakfast. At this point you can see that they are getting to know each other. They continue to laugh together as they drive. Liz is "uneasy" with her father being a hunter--she's not used to it-as they walk through the woods. When she says, "Daddy,' I ask shyly, 'were you scared in the war?'" it leads to a good conversation between them. . . . At the end they are becoming dad and daughter because the story ends with "Then I put it into the pocket of my shirt and reach over out of my enormous cuff, and take my father's hand.'

Back Up Your Thinking

Name: _____   Date: _____

Title: _____

```
                        ┌─────────────────┐
                        │   My thinking   │
                        │                 │
                        └─────────────────┘
                                 │
                                 ▼
┌─────────────────┐     ┌─────────────────┐     ┌─────────────────┐
│   My thinking   │     │    Evidence     │     │   My thinking   │
│                 │     │                 │     │                 │
└─────────────────┘     │                 │     └─────────────────┘
         │              └─────────────────┘              │
         ▼                       │                       ▼
┌─────────────────┐             ▼              ┌─────────────────┐
│    Evidence     │                            │    Evidence     │
│                 │     ╭─────────────────╮    │                 │
│                 │     │ An observation  │    │                 │
└─────────────────┘     │ about the text  │    └─────────────────┘
         ▼              │ (character,     │            ◄
                        │ event, theme,   │
                        │ etc.)           │
                        │                 │
                        ╰─────────────────╯
```

Helpful phrases for citing evidence:

According to the text . . .

The author said . . .

Based on. . . .

For example . . .

For instance . . .

From the reading, I know . . .

It said on page . . .

A quote that shows this is . . .

This demonstrates _____ because . . .

This is evident because . . .

This proves because . . .

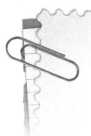

EXCERPT TO WRITE ABOUT

"Saturday at the Canal"

by Gary Soto

▶ **This is from a collection of stories called** *Leaving Home: 15 Distinguished Authors Explore Personal Journeys.* **As you read this poem, think about why it belongs in the collection. What specific details or evidence makes you think that?**

I was hoping to be happy by seventeen.

School was a sharp check mark in the roll book,

An obnoxious tuba playing at noon because our team

Was going to win at night. The teachers were

Too close to dying to understand. The hallways

Stank of poor grades and unwashed hair. Thus,

A friend and I sat watching the water on Saturday,

Neither of us talking much, just warming ourselves

By hurling large rocks at the dusty ground

And feeling awful because San Francisco was a postcard

On a bedroom wall. We wanted to go there,

Hitchhike under the last migrating birds

And be with people who knew more than three chords

On a guitar. We didn't drink or smoke,

But our hair was shoulder length, wild when

The wind picked up and the shadows of

This loneliness gripped loose dirt. By bus or car,

By the sway of train over a long bridge,

We wanted to get out. The years froze

As we sat on the bank. Our eyes followed the water,

White-tipped but dark underneath, racing out of town.

Source: "Saturday at the Canal" from *A Fire in My Hands: Poems* by Gary Soto. Copyright © 1999, 2006 by Gary Soto. Reprinted by permission of Houghton Mifflin Harcourt Publishing company. All rights reserved.

Note: Like any work of art, there is no single correct answer about this poem's meaning. What I like about it is that even students in the intermediate grades can pick up the theme of longing and the moments of boredom and disengagement in childhood. Students in Grades 5 and above may be able to relate more to the dreams of one day growing up and out of one's hometown. The power of the asking questions work is that by scribbling lots of questions in the margins, students open up opportunities for discussion. You might seek answers to questions about the specifics of the narrator and his friend. (Why San Francisco? Why did they dislike school? When was this poem written relative to being 17?) Or questions and evidence related to Soto's use of imagery or the setting.

Quote From the Text

BEST THE TEST

On standardized tests, students often must choose the line that supports the answer to a question. In Grades 5 and up, they are asked to provide quotes. You can:

- Provide practice with this skill, throughout the year, orally and in writing.

- To keep the skill-building authentic, have your *students* come up with a question that dogs them as they read. Then they can "lift a line" or pull a longer quote that supports their question and write about it.

LESSON PREP

- Choose chapter books that lend themselves to powerful questions from the outset. Read and familiarize yourself with these books. If you can have students reading entire chapter books, that is optimal, or you can practice with the excerpt provided here.

- Photocopy Question, Quote, Write! (page 24) and the excerpt from *The Giver* (page 25).

INTRODUCE IT

1. Model how readers ask questions as they begin a book and how these questions are based on the text rather than random musings. Think aloud how you "lift out" the sentence or passage and use it to respond to your question.

2. Ask students to do the same, working with one question, a quote that supports their answer, and why it supports it.

3. Using one of the excerpts, guide students through this process, allowing them to create their own questions and find quotes.

For ELLs and students who may need extra support, use the Quote From the Text to Answer Questions form at **http://resources.corwin.com/ evidencebasedwriting-fiction.**

The Giver by Lois Lowry (or any of the books in that series)

Out of the Dust by Karen Hesse

The Music of Dolphins by Karen Hesse

Hatchet by Gary Paulsen

Hapless Hamster: https://youtu.be/w1aDcjqYBNI

Pigeons: https://youtu.be/oIllVFBBbNw

WRITE-ABOUT-READING TEMPLATE

GRAB & GO

Quote From the Text to Answer Questions

Name: _____ Date: _____

Title: _____

Directions:

- Pretend you are writing a question for a test that has to be answered using a quote from the text.
- Write a question from the text you are reading and then write the answer, including a direct quote or exact lines from the text.

Question:
_____
_____
_____

The answer to the question is _____
_____
_____
_____
_____

I know this because in the text it says, "_____
_____
_____
_____
_____"

An interview on how Lois Lowry got the idea for *The Giver:* http://www.npr.org/2014/08/16/340170478/ lois-lowry-says-the-giver-was-inspired-by-her-fathers-memory-loss

HOW TO USE THE GRAB AND GO PAGES

- Distribute to students copies of Question, Quote, Write! on page 24 and the Lois Lowry novel excerpt on page 25.

- Students read through the text once, then reread following the directions at the end of the excerpt.

- Students then pose a question and go back through the excerpt to highlight specific lines of text that would lead them to ask that question.

- Guide students if they need your help at first. Break it into steps: asking questions, then sharing, then highlighting and annotating text and sharing their thinking—either through turn and talk or small groups.

- After finishing the text, students use the Question, Quote, Write! template to record their question, lift a line or a quote, and then respond by writing about their thinking. (They may need teacher direction when they get to the "write about your thinking" prompt. Instead of using the write-about-reading template, this can be easily done in their reading journals.)

- **Ongoing:** Find other great excerpts that students can go through this process with; ask students' permission if you want to use their responses as mentor texts in future lessons.

- Once students are comfortable with asking questions, citing evidence, and finding quotes or lifting lines, it becomes a natural part of responding to reading. However, be judicious with this. Practice is great, but if you sense students are tiring of writing these short responses, move on!

SAMPLE TO SHARE WITH STUDENTS

Question, Quote, Write!

Name Kate

Title Cheyenne Again

A question you have from reading the text:

Why does Young Bull have to go to school and learn to be a white man?

"Lift a line"
(Quote from the text!)

"But no, Young Bull must leave. Now is the white man's world."

"The corn is drying out. There will be food at this place they call school."

Respond: write about your *thinking about the question and the quote:*

Young Bull had to go to school because back then, bording schools forced young Indians to attend, even against the parents will. The schools goals were too make the children forget their culture. One schools motto was "from savagery into civilization." Once the Indian finished school, they did not get to go back to their parents. The mood of this book was defenetly mad!

Question, Quote, Write!

Name: _____   Date: _____

Title: _____

A question you have from reading the text:

_____

_____

_____

_____

"Lift a line" (quote from the text):

_____

_____

_____

_____

Respond: Write about your thinking about the question and the quote:

_____

_____

_____

_____

_____

_____

_____

_____

_____

_____

_____

_____

_____

Available for download at **http://resources.corwin.com/evidencebasedwriting-fiction**

EXCERPT TO WRITE ABOUT

The Giver

by Lois Lowry

▶ On the first page of *The Giver*, Jonas, the main character, is beginning to feel frightened and he compares that to how he felt when he saw a plane fly overhead. After the plane had passed overhead multiple times, the community loudspeakers ordered everyone inside.

[pp. 2–3]

He had been frightened then. The sense of his own community silent, waiting, had made his stomach churn. He had trembled.

But it had been nothing. Within minutes the speakers had crackled again, and the voice, reassuring now and less urgent, had explained that a Pilot-in-Training had misread his navigational instructions and made a wrong turn. Desperately the Pilot had been trying to make his way back before his error was noticed.

NEEDLESS TO SAY, HE WILL BE RELEASED, the voice had said, followed by silence. There was an ironic tone to that final message, as if the Speaker found it amusing and Jonas had smiled a little, though he knew what a grim statement it had been. For a contributing citizen to be released from the community was a final decision, a terrible punishment, an overwhelming statement of failure.

Even the children were scolded if they used the term lightly at play, jeering at a teammate who missed a catch or stumbled in a race. Jonas had done it once, had shouted at his best friend, "That's it, Asher! You're released!" when Asher's clumsy error had lost a match for his team. He had been taken aside for a brief and serious talk by the coach, had hung his head with guilt and embarrassment, and apologized to Asher after the game.

Are there any words in this excerpt that are used in an unusual way? What does that make you wonder/question?

Look at the font and size of font. When an author uses all capitals, that is something to pay attention to. What does that make you wonder/question?

Reread the text and think about anything that doesn't appear "normal." Highlight the sections that make you wonder and jot notes of your thinking in the margin.

Then use the Question, Quote, Write! sheet to record one question you are asking after reading this text and why you're asking it. What in the text led you to ask this question?

Note: Lois Lowry opens her novel with a scene that makes readers work hard to figure out what is going on. It's not a warm, familiar scene, with details of children playing on green grass. Instead, a disembodied voice on a loud speaker, formal words like *citizen* and *community*. What other words are off-putting?

Summarize in Literature

Summary: Identifies the key ideas, details, or events in the text and reports them with an emphasis on who did what to whom and when. In other words, the emphasis is on retelling what happened or what the text says with the utmost fidelity to the text itself, thus requiring students to check what they say against what the text says happened.

Objective Summary (Grades 6–8): This describes key ideas details or events in the text and reports them without adding any commentary or outside description. It is similar to an evening "recap" of the news that attempts to answer the reporter's essential questions—who, what where, when, why, and how—without commentary.

PROMPTS FOR SUMMARIZING IN LITERATURE

- What details from the beginning, middle, and end would I include in a summary on this text?

- What details and information must an objective summary of the text include?

 Available for download at **http://resources.corwin.com/evidencebasedwriting-fiction**

BEST THE TEST

Summarizing is a key comprehension skill. Think aloud for students how you summarize, and write on chart paper so students see how to summarize in writing.

- Understanding chronology is an important aspect of summarizing.

- Transition words are also a part of summarizing, and using them comes into play on standardized tests.

- To summarize something is to narrow it down to the most important details, in the order they occur. A summary is more sharply focused than a retelling.

LESSON PREP

- Choose a book with a distinct plot and chronology. Eve Bunting's *Gleam and Glow* is a great one.

INTRODUCE IT

1. Distribute prompts to students and/or display them on a wall as an anchor chart.

2. Also create your own anchor chart with the prompts.

3. Have an anchor chart with transitional words available to reference.

4. Before reading, tell students that they are going to summarize the book, not retell it. As you read, you are going to mark pages that have information important to the story (4 × 6 sticky notes are great for this).

5. Read the book, stop, and discuss important junctures and mark them (hitting characters, setting, problems, events, ending). (Possible junctures are pp. 1, 3, 7, 11, 15, 17, 19, 23, 25, 27.) This is a book about refugees fleeing war with a definite chronology and ending.

6. When finished, create a chart labeled Beginning, Middle, and End. While simple summaries start with five sentences, more sophisticated summaries include more detail and cite evidence. Depending on the grade you teach, and other factors, start simple or add more detail.

7. Revisit the sticky notes and jot on the chart, filling in the characters and setting in the beginning,

along with the problem. Fill in at least three important events in the middle, then finish with the end. It helps to number the events to show sequence.

8. **Write about reading:** Once you have the chart filled out, co-construct a summary, either on chart paper or typed to be photocopied and distributed for students to refer to. Depending on the grade level, lift lines and cite evidence in the summary.

9. Tell students they will be practicing summaries about the books they read. (See the following example.)

> ## Gleam and Glow
> by Eve Bunting
> ### Purpose - Co-constructed Summary
>
> Gleam and Glow is a story about families fleeing war. While the story never states the country, the afterword says it's Bosnia-Herzegovina in 1990. Victor, the son, tells the story. After his father leaves to fight in the "underground", Victor, Marina (his sister) and his mother have to leave their home because "enemies were coming, sweeping through villages like brooms, forcing people out, and burning their homes." People② leaving the country stopped by their house for food and to rest. One③ day a man left two fish in a bowl behind. Marina named the fish Gleam and Glow. When it's time for the family to leave, they can't carry the fish, so Victor puts them in the pond. As they④ leave their home, Victor wonders, "Would we ever come home again? Would Papa ever find us?" They walk and walk for many days until they reach the border and the camp for people fleeing. Finally, after a long time, Papa finds them there. Months later it's safe to go home. When they return everything is destroyed. Marina remembers Gleam and Glow and they find the pond full of fish. This has the message of the book: "In spite of everything, they lived. "Mama whispered. Like us, I thought, They lived." The family lived in spite of everything and had come back home.

To learn more about Eve Bunting: http://www.scholastic.com/teachers/contributor/eve-bunting

Background on the war from *Gleam and Glow*: https://history.state.gov/milestones/1993-2000/bosnia

Any high-interest texts fit the bill, but here are a couple to get you started!

- *Cheyenne Again* by Eve Bunting
- *Back of the Bus* by Aaron Reynolds

To practice summarizing, use these short clips:

- Sequencing: The Hapless Hamster: https://youtu.be/w1aDcjqYBNI
- An interview with Eve Bunting: http://www.readingrockets.org/books/interviews/bunting

HOW TO USE THE GRAB AND GO PAGES

- Distribute to students copies of the Arachne myth on page 31 and Summary Planner on page 30.

- Either independently, with partners, or in small groups, have students read and annotate the myth and highlight important points.

- Next, students fill out the Summary Planner.

- Finally, students use the planner to help them write a summary. (It's fine for students to use the co-constructed piece as a model.)

- **On another day**: Have students read and summarize picture books or short stories using the same process described above.

- **Ongoing:** As students become more adept at summaries, add to the requirements. For example, you could have them cite evidence; ask them to highlight the evidence with a highlighter marker.

MORE TEMPLATES TO SHARE WITH STUDENTS

 Available for download at **http://resources.corwin.com/evidencebasedwriting-fiction**

Arachne, the Little Spinner

This myth explains how the spider came to be. It starts in Athens, Greece, which was dedicated to Athena, the goddess of wisdom. Arachne lived in Athens and she was beautiful and a beautiful weaver. For example, "Her hair was like spun gold, and her face was very fair to look upon." She was famous for her weaving and no one could compare to her. That made her boastful. One day a nymph asked Arachne about her weaving and Arachne boasted that "she excelled even Athena herself." She even went on to say, "Athena taught me not. I taught myself." Her friends went off and told the story, but Athena continued to spin. That night an old lady came and asked if she was "jesting" and then said, "You do not mean to compare yourself with Athena?" Arachne stuck to her story and the old woman told her she had offended Athena. Arachne refused to apologize and instead said Athena should have a weaving contest with her. The old woman was Athena and they set up the contest. They met on the shores of the sea, and gods, goddesses and others watched. Both Arachne and Athena spun beautiful "webs" but Athena's was full of "truth and beauty." And Arachne's wasn't entirely truthful about the gods, but still beautiful. When both were held up, Arachne had lost, but she still didn't apologize to Athena. Athena told her the lesson, "Ah, Arachne, there is no pleasure in working for others unless truth and beauty enter into all which we do." Athena turned Arachne into a spider, but she still shows us what a beautiful web she wove long ago.

GRAB & GO

Summary Planner

Name: _____   Date: _____

Title: _____

Beginning	
Characters	**Problem(s)**

Middle
1.
2.
3.

End

EXCERPT TO WRITE ABOUT

"The Mythical Story of Arachne"
by Emma M. Firth

Athena, the goddess of wisdom, taught the Grecian people the useful arts, and they honored her by giving to her the care of one of their fairest cities, Athens. In this beautiful city they built the Parthenon and dedicated it to Athena. In the temple they placed a statue of the goddess. It was made of ivory and gold, and its robes were spun, woven, and embroidered by the fairest maidens in Greece.

The Greek maidens all knew how to spin and embroider. They said that Athena taught them. It would have been wrong to think otherwise.

One day a Grecian maiden sat spinning beneath an olive-tree on the shore of the blue Aegean Sea. She was a pretty picture. Her hair was like spun gold, and her face was very fair to look upon. She held her head high, and turned it somewhat haughtily when a sly little nymph, who had been watching, asked her about her work. The little maid was Arachne, the most skillful spinner in Greece. None could equal her in the weaving of beautiful webs; and her fame had gone abroad, for the webs which Arachne wove and embroidered with her nimble fingers were sent far away, to be worn by the great people of other lands.

Everybody praised the little maid so lavishly that they quite turned her head. It was unfortunate indeed that a maiden so charming in most respects should not be agreeable in all; but the foolish little Arachne was so much given to boasting of herself and of her skill that she was at times far from agreeable. At such times the little nymphs, who stole softly near to watch her as her slender finders flew deftly to and fro, ran back to their vines and streams, while her friends grew weary and left her alone.

One day Arachne made a foolish boast. She declared that she excelled even Athena herself.

"O Arachne, Arachne, how wicked! Why, Athena taught you all you know," cried her friends.

But the vain little maiden shook her pretty head, saying, "Athena taught me not. I taught myself."

Arachne's friends were shocked. They went home at once, while the naughty Arachne, with a toss of her proud little head, went on spinning and spinning.

By and by a shadow fell across the snowy wool, and looking up, Arachne saw an old woman leaning on her staff.

"My daughter, I heard that remark. It was foolish; but you are young, and perchance were jesting. You do not mean to compare yourself with Athena?"

"Yes, I do," said Arachne, still spinning.

"Then you have greatly offended the goddess, and should beg her pardon."

"I do not care. Do you suppose that Athena could weave a mantle finer than this?" And Arachne held up a soft scarf, rich with Tyrian purple and gold. "Let Athena come and try, if she thinks she can do better. I will match my skill with hers."

As Arachne said this, the cloak fell from the old woman's shoulders, and the stately goddess Athena stood before her. But Arachne was not abashed. She refused to ask pardon, and insisted upon a trial of skill.

They met on the shores of the sea, while the sea nymphs, the tritons, and Arachne's friends watched anxiously. Never before had a mortal dared to vie with a goddess; and everyone knew that, should Arachne fail, her punishment would be severe. So they watched, almost breathlessly, as the hands of the spinners deftly carded the soft, fine wool, then twisted it into threads. Then these threads were stretched on frames, and soon the shuttles flew back and forth as if by magic.

(Continued)

(Continued)

Athena wove into her web the colors of the rainbow, and more beautiful pictures than mortal eyes had ever beheld. She made pictures of the gods, Zeus seated on his throne, with the stately Hera, and all the gods and goddesses in attendance; Helios in his chariot; Proserpine with her garlands of flowers; and the seagod, Poseidon, with his trident. There was truth and beauty in every line of Athena's web.

Arachne's web was also beautiful, but it was not entirely truthful, for her pictures were those which showed the errors and failings of others.

When Athena's web was finished, Zephyrus bore it aloft, and stretched it across the sky in a beautiful arch. But Arachne's web grew darker and darker. She knew that she was beaten, but would not ask forgiveness of the now angry Athena, who struck the web and rent it. Arachne snatched the fragments, and would have strangled herself; but Athena said, "Ah, Arachne, there is no pleasure in working for others unless truth and beauty enter into all which we do. That which is done for self-praise is wrong. You shall live to warn people who boast of their skill rather than make it a means of doing good." Then she touched Arachne; and, sad to tell, her beautiful hair fell off, her body shriveled, and she turned into a spider. But she still shows us how wonderful a web she wove in those days of long ago.

Note: Greek myths offer fabulous opportunities to read and write about character traits, because clearly, those gods and goddesses lived large! In this telling of the Arachne myth, the take-away lesson is clearly stated: "That which is done for self-praise is wrong." As a classroom activity, have students read myths about Athena, Poseidon, and others. A good compare-and-contrast task would be to look at the three versions of the Arachne myth.

Cite Evidence That Provides an Analysis

BEST THE TEST

Short stories and movies are often used on standardized tests for summarizing tasks. Guide students to pay attention and read the question carefully, because sometimes you're supposed to summarize the setting—not the plot! Other pointers:

- Students are asked to find a certain number of examples, or lines *from the text,* to include in their written response. That's why having students highlight evidence they are using in their summaries is great practice.

- Students in sixth through eighth grades should practice writing objective summaries about their reading (see page 26). However, this should not preclude writing personal responses about their thinking. Be explicit that one is a test strategy and the other is a life strategy.

LESSON PREP

- Photocopy the Summary Planner template (page 30) and the story excerpts by Francisco Jimenez (page 36).

- These excerpts are divided into beginning, middle events, and ending and lend themselves to summarizing.

- Have the entire short story, "The Circuit," available for each student. It is included in *The Circuit: Stories From the Life of a Migrant Child* by Francisco Jimenez.

INTRODUCE IT

1. Read aloud the entire "The Circuit," and model just for a minute or two how you hold your thinking about important details in the story's beginning, using sticky note jots or annotating in the margins.

2. Quickly turn the work over to students, having them do this same process as they move through the story's beginning, middle, and end. This story lends itself to inferential thinking, so have students mark where they are making inferences and the details (phrases, sentences) that support it.

3. Have students get in pairs or small groups to support one another as they fill out the Summary Planner. Circulate and prompt as needed to help them decide the most important parts to include in a summary.

4. Have students number or annotate to help them with sequence.

5. For homework or on another day, students can use these notes to write a summary, including evidence from the text.

To learn more about Francisco Jimenez: http://www.scholastic.com/teachers/contributor/francisco-jimenez

A wonderful companion text to "The Circuit" is the picture book *La Mariposa* by Francisco Jimenez. This book could be used in a first lesson and then compared/contrasted with the short story "Inside Out" in *The Circuit: Stories From the Life of a Migrant Child* by Francisco Jimenez.

Myths, folktales, and short stories are all excellent for modeling summaries and citing evidence.

Francisco Jimenez video on growing up a migrant child: https://youtu.be/cWL2d_NYLKc

HOW TO USE THE GRAB AND GO PAGES

- Here are two options for using "The Circuit" by Francisco Jimenez and the Cite Evidence Choice Board on page 35:

  o **Option 1:** Use as a teacher-guided lesson. After you have read aloud the entire short story, have students use either the Summary Planner from Lesson 5 or the Cite Evidence Choice Board to notice and annotate the excerpts from "The Circuit" and write a summary.

  o **Option 2:** Use the entire "The Circuit" and the Summary Planner as small-group or individual practice for students. Direct students to read the story *and stop at the passages on the excerpt page* to discuss which lines to include in an objective summary, and why.

- Students then each draft an objective summary, citing evidence.

- **On another day:** Have students share their summaries and discuss. (Summaries should be similar if students have included salient details.)

- Have students complete the second part of the task—the response.

- **Ongoing:** As you finish shared novels or class books, use it as an opportunity to practice summarizing. However, as always, when you sense your students have "got it," ease up on summarizing and focus more on response.

- Use the Cite Evidence Choice Board to give students practice with all the aspects of close reading or to practice summarizing.

Cite Evidence Choice Board

Find two important quotes from the text. Explain them.	What was an important question you had? Why was it important and what was the answer?	What was an inference you made and the details that supported it?
How? Write a question from your reading that starts with "How" and then write the answer.	**Title** _____ _____ **Author** _____	**Why?** Write a question from your reading that starts with "Why" and then write the answer.
What? What was the most important event? How do you know this?	**Who?** Write a question from your reading that starts with "Who" and then write the answer.	**Where and When?** Write a question from your reading that starts with "Where and when" and then write the answer.

Available for download at **http://resources.corwin.com/evidencebasedwriting-fiction**

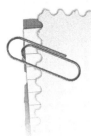

EXCERPTS TO WRITE ABOUT

"The Circuit"

From *The Circuit: Stories From the Life of a Migrant Child*

by Francisco Jimenez

▶ **As you read through these excerpts, highlight lines that would be important to include in a summary. Jot your thinking in the margin.**

Beginning [pp. 73–74]

It was that time of year again. Ito, the strawberry sharecropper, did not smile. It was natural. The peak of the strawberry season was over and the last few days the workers, most of them braceros, were not picking as many boxes as they had during the months of June and July.

As the last days of August disappeared, so did the number of braceros. Sunday, only one—the best picker—came to work. I liked him. Sometimes we talked during our half-hour lunch break. That is how I found out he was from Jalisco, the same state in Mexico my family was from. That Sunday was the last time I saw him.

When the sun had tired and sunk behind the mountains, Ito signaled us that it was time to go home. "Ya esora," he yelled in his broken Spanish. Those were the words I waited for twelve hours a day, every day, seven days a week, week after week. And the thought of not hearing them again saddened me.

As we drove home, Papa did not say a word. With both hands on the wheel, he stared at the dirt road. My older brother, Roberto, was also silent. He leaned his head back and closed his eyes. Once in a while he cleared from his throat the dust that blew in from outside.

Yes, it was that time of year. When I opened the front door to the shack, I stopped. Everything we owned was neatly packed in cardboard boxes. Suddenly I felt even more the weight of hours, days, weeks, and months of work. I sat down on a box. The thought of having to move to Fresno and knowing what was in store for me there brought tears to my eyes.

That night I could not sleep. I lay in bed thinking about how much I hated this move.

▶ **What would be important to include in a summary from this beginning? Hint: These characters are migrant workers picking strawberries, and it seems the season is over and they have to move. But remember, a summary includes not only what is literally occurring—but also the characters' responses to the events.**

Middle *The next morning the family packed the car and drove to Fresno.* [pp. 76–77]

As we drove away, I felt a lump in my throat. I turned around and looked at our little shack for the last time.

At sunset we drove into a labor camp near Fresno. Since Papa did not speak English, Mama asked the camp foreman if he needed any more workers. "We don't need no more," said the foreman, scratching his head. "Check with Sullivan down the road, Can't miss him. He lives in a big white house with a fence around it."

(Continued)

When we got there, Mama walked up to the house. . . .

"We have work! Mr. Sullivan said we can stay there the whole season," she said, gasping and pointing to an old garage near the stables.

The garage was worn out by the years. It had no windows. The walls, eaten by termites, strained to support the roof full of holes. The dirt floor, populated by earth worms, looked like a gray road map.

▶ **What is important from this section that would be included in a summary? Highlight and jot notes about why it's important.**

▶ **The family moves in and cleans and the next day Papa, Roberto, and the author go to work in fields. The author continues to work in the fields.**

[pp. 80–81]

It was Monday, the first week of November. The grape season was over and I could now go to school. I woke up early that morning and lay in bed, looking at the stars and savoring the thought of not going to work and of starting sixth grade for the first time that year. . . .

When Papa and Roberto left for work, I felt relief. I walked to the top of a small grade next to the shack and watch the Carcahita disappear in a cloud of dust.

Two hours later, around eight o'clock, I stood by the side of the road waiting for school bus number twenty. When it arrived I climbed in. I sat in an empty seat in the back.

When the bus stopped in front of the school, I felt very nervous. I looked out the bus window and saw boys and girls carrying books under their arms. I put my hands in my pant pockets and walked to the principal's office.

▶ **Look back through this section. What is important to remember? Highlight and jot notes.**

▶ **The author is assigned to Mr. Lema's sixth-grade classroom where the teacher gives him an English book.**

[pp. 82–83]

"Would you like to read?" he asked hesitantly. I opened the book to page 125. My mouth was dry. My eyes began to water. I could not begin. "You can read later," Mr. Lema said understandingly.

▶ **The author goes to the restroom during recess and attempts to read the book; however; there were so many words he didn't know. He heads back to the classroom.**

Mr. Lema was sitting at this desk correcting papers. When I entered he looked up at me and smiled. I felt better. I walked up to him and asked if he could help me with the new words. "Gladly," he said.

The rest of the month I spent my lunch hours working on English with Mr. Lema, my best friend at school.

▶ **Has the narrator changed? What happened to make that change? How would that be important to include in a summary?**

Ending [p. 83]

One Friday during lunch hour, Mr. Lema asked me to take a walk with him to the music room. "Do you like music?" he asked me as we entered the building. "Yes, I like

(Continued)

corridos," I answered. He then picked up a trumpet, blew on it, and handed it to me. The sound gave me goose bumps. I knew that sound. I had heard it in many *corridos*. "How would you like to learn how to play it?" he asked. He must have read my face because before I could answer, he added, "I'll teach you how to play it during our lunch hours."

That day I could hardly wait to tell Papa and Mama the great news. As I got off the bus, my little brothers and sister ran up to meet me. They were yelling and screaming. I thought they were happy to see me, but when I opened the door to our shack, I saw that everything we owned was neatly packed in cardboard boxes.

▶ **Think about the end of this section. What are you left thinking? What are you thinking will happen? What is important from this section to include in the summary?**

Tasks: **Choose one!**

1. Summary: Write an *objective* summary of your reading.

2. Response: Write a *response to the text.* What are you thinking as you read this? What are you wondering? What opinion do you have and why?

Note: The title "The Circuit" refers to the circuit and cycle that migrant workers go through as they pick cotton, strawberries, grapes, and other crops. In this story, students get a glimpse of the physical labor and emotional hardship of immigrants. The author writes about his experience of being a child of illegal immigrants in a manner that is timeless. What accounts for the timelessness? For one thing, an absence of pop culture references. Although the setting is in the early 1950s, it could be today. You might want to find current news stories about the Mexican border and immigration in print and online, and have students compare and contrast points of view with this story.

SECTION 2

Relationships

Relationships are the heart of fiction. In this set of lessons we look at how authors use techniques to convey characters on a page to keep us reading. One of my favorite writers is Pat Conroy, and in an interview in 2010 on National Public Radio, he told of how his mother would read him stories at bedtime, and when reading aloud *Gone With the Wind*, she likened all the main characters to relatives. He said it made him aware that life and art are close, and our job as readers is to pay attention to how the novelist is making that close connection matter. We read fiction to understand ourselves and other people in our lives.

For elementary school students, I've found it helpful to come at introducing character relationships in fiction through the pathways of setting and sequence of events/ plot. Why? It's concrete, and students more easily get that the parade of events are the "movie reels" in their heads as they read.

On standardized tests, when students have to pencil in, drag and drop, write about characters in terms of cause and effect, compare and contrast, and such, all the warm, engaging reading and talking you do all year with your students will have been the best "test prep" in the world. Yes, reading *volumes* of books and responding in authentic

ways will transfer to testing situations, because students will understand how cause and effect works in literature by racking up the sky miles of many novels, and their plot twists built on the seismic shifts in human relationships.

To understand relationships in books, *students need to hold their thinking over time*. The lessons in this section teach them to analyze, revisit, reread, and reflect. They offer students opportunities to respond in writing, during and after reading, using write-about-reading templates to scaffold and do short stop and jots. The goal is to get our students writing about their reading independently and choosing the tools that work *for them*.

As you present these lessons and invent your own, embrace character *change*: Get beyond over-focusing on static traits and ask students: How did the character come off in Chapter 1? What is different about her in Chapter 5, and why? What about her is changed in Chapter 10? What is your theory about the character? How do setting and plot affect that? Discuss elements of narrative, including setting, characters (including the terms *protagonist* and *antagonist*), plot (review terms such as *climax* and *resolution*), and sequence of events often in class so students transfer this know-how to testing situations.

Watch Leslie Teach!

Video 2: **Watch students engage in small-group novel discussions focused on character change and conflict.**

Go to **http://resources.corwin.com/evidencebasedwriting-fiction** to see the lessons and guided practice in action.

Describe Characters, Setting, and Sequence

Character: Characters can be simple (flat, static, like Judy Moody) or complex (round, dynamic, like August in *Wonder*). To be complex, characters need to change, possess conflicting traits or needs, and have a rich inner life that kind of combusts as the person interacts with others and his or her environment. The character's journey is often represented as an arc: What they are like or where they are when the story *begins* and when it *ends*.

Character Traits: The personality and behaviors as well as the physical attributes of a character. As the character emerges, different traits can be revealed through stated or implied motivations and feelings, thoughts, words, and actions.

Setting: The place or time in which a story, novel, or drama takes place. The setting can augment character and plot in providing a social, economic, cultural backdrop. It can add to the mood or tone of the story, too.

Sequence of Events: The order that events in a story or text occur in the order that specific tasks are performed. Like setting, the sequence of events in a narrative creates the passage of time in a story.

PROMPTS FOR DESCRIBING CHARACTERS, SETTING, AND SEQUENCE

- What do I know *literally* about the character physically and emotionally?

- What can I *infer*?

- When I visualize the setting of important scenes, what does that reveal about the characters?

- What details about nature, weather, and physical surroundings is the author providing? Why?

- What does a character's relationship with objects suggest about the character?

- What does he think, feel, say, or do that gives clues?

- How does the main character try to solve her problem?

- What is the sequence of events in the story?

- What do you notice about the passage of time?

 Available for download at
http://resources.corwin.com/evidencebasedwriting-fiction

BEST THE TEST

"Drag and drop" is a common test task/format. Students often have to select trait words describing characters or drag and drop to sequence major events. Tips:

- Provide students with practice using highly varied vocabulary for character traits.

- Make students aware that follow-up questions require choosing lines from the text to support their choices. Give them practice highlighting and annotating texts so that choosing evidence becomes second nature to them.

- Get students accustomed to providing written explanations about some aspect of character and setting that include direct quotes and other examples from the text.

- Make discussion of story characters related to setting a natural part of literacy instruction.

- Discuss setting routinely so students can describe *where* a story takes place (there may be more than one setting) and *when* it takes place, whether it's a specific time period or *past, present,* or *future.* Encourage students to consider the setting's effect on the mood of the protagonist.

LESSON PREP

- Photocopy Look @ Literary Elements on page 46 and "The Shepherd's Mistake" on page 47.

- Choose a book with strong characters. (I use Patricia Polacco's *Thank You, Mr. Falker* for this model lesson.) Place sticky notes on pages that contain stated and implied clues to character so students operate both literally and inferentially (e.g., p. 3, "Still she loved being in school because she could draw." "'In first grade, you'll learn to read,' her brother said." shows actions about her abilities; p. 6. "Trisha began to feel 'different.' She began to feel dumb." shows her feelings and how she views herself).

- Create an anchor chart for literary elements similar to the reproducible on page 46, which you will use later in the lesson.

INTRODUCE IT

1. Distribute prompts to students and/or display them on a wall as an anchor chart.

2. Also create your own anchor chart with the prompts.

3. Read *Thank You, Mr. Falker* (or another book with rich character development), and do a think-aloud at the spots you have flagged. (Possible junctures are pp. 8, 11, 15, 17, 20, 24, 30, 31, 34.)

4. Call attention to the illustrations, too, so that students can also *infer* or determine what the main character looks like, and keep referring to your anchor chart.

5. As you stop to discuss your sticky notes have students help you *code* them **T** for thoughts, **F** for feelings, **A** for actions, and **W** for words.

6. After finishing the book, ask: What is the setting? Fill in the anchor chart. (The story starts in Michigan and moves to California. It takes place in the past; pictures help determine that. And the story is mostly in the classroom over a period of years.)

7. Model how you revisit your sticky notes to determine the most important information to transfer to the character description part of the chart.

8. Finally, review the book and fill out the important events flow chart. Starting with the beginning, add at least three major events and the ending (resolution).

9. **Write about reading:** Co-construct a paragraph that *explains* the main character. Make sure to use *specific trait words* (not *nice* or *good*). Start a new anchor chart of positive and negative trait words. This extends vocabulary for English language learners (ELLs) and transfers to testing situations.

10. Tell students that they will be doing the same process you are now modeling, answering the questions: What is the setting? How can I describe the main character? What are the important events in the story? (Sequence)

For more information on Patricia Polacco:
http://www.patriciapolacco.com

For students who may need more scaffolding, download the Character Summarizer and Setting Summarizer at **http://resources.corwin .com/evidencebasedwriting-fiction**.

Any books by Patricia Polacco are win-win, because her illustrations help convey setting.

A Bad Case of Stripes by David Shannon

Wilfred Gordon MacDonald Partridge by Mem Fox

Any books by Roald Dahl provide vivid character descriptions.

Picture books rich for setting:

- *Amber on the Mountain* by Tony Johnston

- *When I Was Young in the Mountains* by Cynthia Rylant

- *See the Ocean* by Estelle Condra

"Glued"—sequence and character traits: https://youtu.be/Vpk7Eje9ZlQ

"Broken Wand"—character traits and comparing two characters: https://youtu.be/Zn3KCceRvfU

An interview with Patricia Polacco: http://www.readingrockets.org/ books/interviews/polacco

HOW TO USE THE GRAB AND GO PAGES

- Distribute to students copies of Look @ Literary Elements on page 46 and "The Shepherd's Mistake" on page 47.

- Either in small groups, with a partner, or independently, students read the folktale and annotate on sticky notes or in the margins.

- Encourage them to *code*.

- Next, have them use their notes to fill out the write-about-reading template.

- Students then use the information to write a paragraph describing the main character, citing examples from the text.

- **On another day**: Have students select another text and do this same process. Over time, the work truly builds students' capacity for writing incisively about texts, using details to bolster their interpretation.

- **Ongoing:** Reuse "The Shepherd's Mistake" to develop your own lessons and practice ideas for looking at plot, theme, or point of view. Like many folktales, it lends itself to an exercise in which students write the story from another character's point of view.

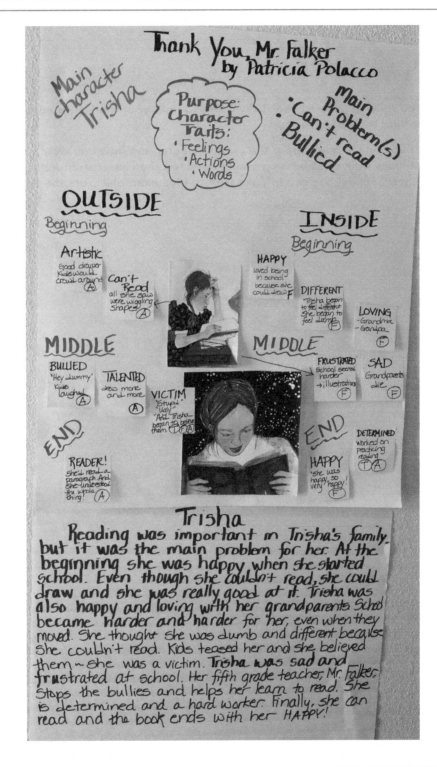

GRAB & GO

Look @ Literary Elements

Name(s): _____

Title: _____

Directions:

- As you read your book, use sticky notes to hold your thinking about characters and important events in the story.

- After you finish, think about the main character and how you would describe him or her. What clues from the text help you understand the character literally, and which ones make you infer? Fill out the chart. Make sure to give examples from the text.

Character:			
Outside (Physical traits)	**Inside:**		
	Thoughts/Feelings	Words (What he or she says)	Actions (What he or she does)
Describe the setting:			
Design a flow chart that sequences the five most important events. You can use a separate sheet of paper or the back of this page.			

EXCERPT TO WRITE ABOUT

"The Shepherd's Mistake"

posted by Brishti Bandyopadhyay in Folktales for Kids

Name: _____ Date: _____

▶ Directions:

- **Read "The Shepherd's Mistake. " Think about character traits.**

- **Read it a second time and highlight lines that help you describe the main character (the shepherd).**

- **Annotate your thinking in the margins using specific character trait words.**

- **Write a paragraph describing the main character.**

Early every morning, a shepherd took his flock of sheep out in the fields to graze. He would sit by watching—as the sheep lazily munched on fresh grass. After they had eaten, he would round them up and walk back home. Sometimes while watching his flock, he would curl up in a quiet corner and go off to sleep.

One day, the shepherd caught a wolf which had strayed into the field, eyeing his sheep. However, it was some distance away and it made no effort to come nearer. The shepherd at first stood on guard against the wolf, as against an enemy, and kept a strict watch over its movements.

But the wolf did not do anything. When the shepherd herded the sheep and headed home with his flock, the wolf quietly followed them at a distance.

This continued for a while. The shepherd would find the wolf waiting at the edge of the field every morning. But it made not the slightest effort to seize the sheep and would just watch. So, by and by, the shepherd let down his guard a

bit. A few days later, he began to actually look forward to the wolf's presence.

The wolf, who generally sat on a large piece of rock, looked like a big sheep dog from afar. The shepherd thought that other wild animals or mischief-makers would be scared of the "dog"'s presence and not harm his flock while it was around.

Now, he began to look upon the wolf as a guardian of his flock. One day, in the middle of grazing his sheep, the shepherd was called back to home urgently. Leaving the sheep entirely in charge of the wolf, he left.

When he came back, what did he find? That the wolf had eaten most of his flock, with only a few sheep wandering about. Carcasses of the dead sheep lay around, everywhere.

The shepherd sat down in shock after witnessing the slaughter. "Serves me right," he moaned to himself, "after all, I entrusted the welfare of my flock to a wolf."

Source: Brishti Bandyopadhyay © Pitara.com

Note: Folktales are short, easily accessible text. Generally the main character displays certain character traits that students can easily discern. In addition, the main character reacts to other characters or situations that students can also identify. Because these are short texts, students can name character traits and cite the text that helps determine these.

Follow Characters, Setting, and Sequence Over Time

BEST THE TEST

Despite the fact that standardized tests rely on short passages, it's the students' ability to "bank" important information and insights across whole texts that serves them well on exams. Focus class discussions and practice on strategies readers use to *sustain* understanding over the course of a short story or chapter book. Specifically:

- Readers need to be open-minded so that as the author plants clues for how characters are evolving and how events can turn things upside down, the reader picks up these clues readily.

- Readers need to become increasingly adept in their ability to compare and contrast characters *within* a book or characters in separate texts.

- Provide students with ample opportunities to read short and longer texts and compare and contrast characters, setting, and other elements.

- Literature circles and book clubs should always include discussion of literary elements so it becomes a natural part of student discourse.

LESSON PREP

- Read a full-length novel or short story so you know it well. (I use *Fish in a Tree* by Lynda Mullaly Hunt in this lesson.) You can either plan to teach the entire novel or just have students work with the excerpts shown on page 52.

- Photocopy Literary Elements Wheel (page 51) and the Lynda Mullaly Hunt story (page 52).

INTRODUCE IT

1. Read aloud the chapter book. Think aloud as you notice setting, character (traits, inner conflict, change), and important events.

2. Demonstrate how you hold your thinking across a chapter book, either with sticky notes, responding in a reader's notebook, or on anchor charts and flow charts.

3. Model how to stop at the end of a chapter and jot thinking about major events and/or character development.

4. If you have less time, use the Literary Elements Wheel.

5. Refer to the anchor chart from Lesson 7 on page 40.

6. As you model, show how your understanding of the character changes over time and *why* it changes.

For more on Lynda Mullaly Hunt: http://www.lyndamullalyhunt.com

Jon Scieszka's books in the Guys Read series are full of short stories for boys as well as girls; they are fabulous collections.

Best Shorts: *Favorite Short Stories for Sharing, Selected by Avi* by Carolyn Shute

The Van Gogh Café by Cynthia Rylant

"One Man Band": https://youtu.be/454nNoD6-TI

HOW TO USE THE GRAB AND GO PAGES

- Distribute to students copies of Literary Elements Wheel on page 51 and the Lynda Mullaly Hunt story on page 52.

  ○ **Option 1:** Have students use the Grab and Go pages to notice and annotate the excerpts on character from *Fish in a Tree* by Lynda Mullaly Hunt. These excerpts include character thoughts and feelings, actions, and dialogue to help the reader infer character traits.

  ○ **Option 2:** Read the entire novel, *Fish in a Tree*, using the Excerpts to Write About as stopping points for student practice. In addition, stop at the end of each chapter and add to thoughts on character. Students can also write responses to these excerpts in their reading journals.

- **On another day:** Have students read Patricia Polacco's *Thank You, Mr. Falker* and compare and contrast the two main characters, Trisha and Ally.

- After they finish reading the book, have students write a summary that includes setting and how the main character changed over the course of the book.

- **Ongoing:** Have students use sticky notes to mark details in their independent reading that support their thinking about the main character, the setting, and important events.

- As students read longer chapter books, have them respond weekly, using the Literary Elements Wheel.

- Use the *Fish in a Tree* excerpts on page 52 as the basis for creating your own excerpts page, covering other key moments in Hunt's novel. For Grades 6–8, put additional focus on the use of *dialogue*.

SAMPLE TO SHARE WITH STUDENTS

Summary of *Have a Hot Time, Hades!*

Hades was a pretty likeable guy: late-night wrestling and Nectar-Cola were the dude's things. Hades was also quite shy, until some goddess of spring "lady," aka Persephone, destroyed his pride and destroyed his macho—even though he was never very macho—everything changed. This Persephone was the daughter of Demeter. Demeter was three things: First, she was overprotective. Second, she was always trying—and *don't* try this at home, kids—to grow plants in Kronos' belly. Third, she was *mean!* Now, I don't know this for sure, but I have to take Mr. God-of-the-Underworld's account of things, because he was in Kronos' stomach...not me. Demeter was another goddess and she had a child and Demeter became an overprotective mom.

One day Hades was making a visit to Earth in his chariot, when he saw Persephone (Demeter's daughter) running towards him. Hades gave a shy smile. Persephone promptly stowed away in his chariot, and sneaked into the underworld, without Hades knowing. Meanwhile, up on Earth, Demeter thought that Hades had kidnapped Persephone, which would bring Hades into a world of hurt. When Hades sent Persephone home, she hosted a picnic during which Cupid, while hiding in the underbrush, pricked Hades with his arrow and made him fall in love with Persephone. Then, Demeter found Hades and punished him "severely," stripping Hades of his pride. This is why Hades is considered evil, but at one time, the gods respected him, and then "BAM!," crushed his pride and made up stories or "myths" to make people think *he* was the bad guy! I'm telling you that he wasn't evil.

Personal response:

I love this book because it tells myths from Hades' point of view and the entire book is hilarious. Plus the author puts in stuff from today (like cell phones, etc.) which makes it even funnier.

Additional summary samples are available for download at
http://resources.corwin.com/evidencebasedwriting-fiction

Literary Elements Wheel

Directions:

- Choose two spokes of the wheel to create a diagonal through the center to help you write about literary elements in the story you're reading.

- Make sure to give examples from the text to explain your thinking.

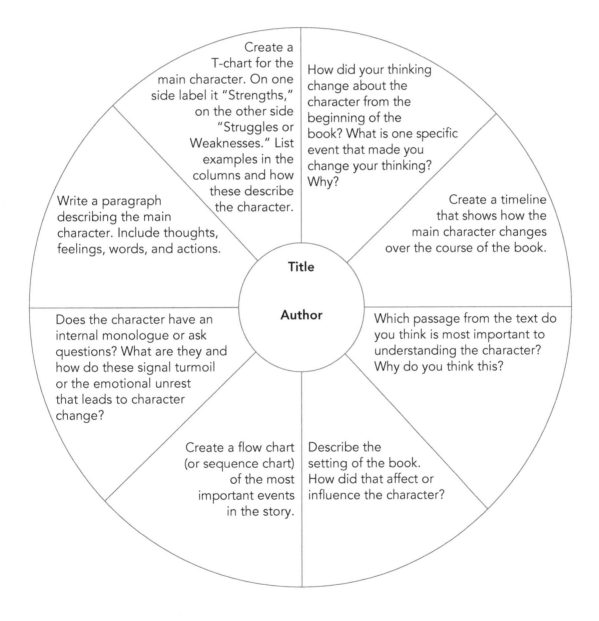

Create a T-chart for the main character. On one side label it "Strengths," on the other side "Struggles or Weaknesses." List examples in the columns and how these describe the character.

How did your thinking change about the character from the beginning of the book? What is one specific event that made you change your thinking? Why?

Write a paragraph describing the main character. Include thoughts, feelings, words, and actions.

Create a timeline that shows how the main character changes over the course of the book.

Title

Author

Does the character have an internal monologue or ask questions? What are they and how do these signal turmoil or the emotional unrest that leads to character change?

Which passage from the text do you think is most important to understanding the character? Why do you think this?

Create a flow chart (or sequence chart) of the most important events in the story.

Describe the setting of the book. How did that affect or influence the character?

EXCERPTS TO WRITE ABOUT

Fish in a Tree

by Lynda Mullaly Hunt

▶ **Chapter 1 is titled "In Trouble Again" and we meet Ally as the teacher asks her to write a one-page paper describing herself. Ally immediately reflects on this.**

[pp. 2–3]

I can't think of anything worse than having to describe myself. I'd rather write about something more positive. Like throwing up at your own birthday party.

"It's important," she says. "It's so your new teacher can get to know you."

. . .

"And," she says, "all that doodling of yours, Ally. If you weren't drawing all the time, your work might be done. Please put it away."

Embarrassed, I slide my drawings underneath my blank writing assignment. I've been drawing pictures of myself being shot out of a cannon. It would be easier than school. Less painful.

"C'mon," she says, moving my lined paper toward me. "Just do your best."

Seven schools in seven years and they're all the same. Whenever I do my best they tell me I don't try hard enough. Too messy. Careless spelling. Annoyed that the same word is spelled different ways on the same page. And the headaches. I always get headaches from looking at the brightness of dark letters on white pages for too long.

Mrs. Hall clears her throat.

The rest of the class is getting tired of me again. Chairs slide. Loud sighs. Maybe they think I can't hear their words: **Freak. Dumb. Loser.**

▶ **As you read this, what are you thinking about Ally? Who is telling the story and how does that affect the point of view? Jot your thinking about Ally, and begin to list some possible character traits. Hint: Think about her thoughts and actions. Consider what others are saying about her.**

▶ **Instead of writing on the paper, Ally scribbles all over her desk. When the teacher threatens to send her to the office *again*, Ally has second thoughts and promises to write.**

[p. 5]

I write with one hand and shield my paper with the other. I know I better keep the pencil moving, so I write the word "Why?" over and over from the top of the page to the very bottom.

(Continued)

One, because I know how to spell it right and two, because I'm hoping someone will finally give me an answer.

▶ **This is the end of the first chapter. What do you know about Ally? What do you wonder? Have you learned about her physical characteristics? Highlight and jot where her thoughts, feelings, and actions provide clues to her inside traits.**

▶ **Mr. Daniels is the replacement for Mrs. Hall and is a unique teacher. Slowly Ally begins to trust him. He acknowledges her gifts and the way she thinks out of the box. However, she continues to be tormented by a few students. When the class goes on a field trip, someone draws a picture of a girl wearing a dunce cap and "Ally" is written underneath. Ally runs away and Mr. Daniels follows.**

[pp. 156–157]

I take a deep breath, and when I let it all out, the words come with it. "Nobody is ever going to be able to help me. Not ever. They all said I should have a dunce cap and they're right. That's the thing. They're right!"

"Oh my . . . Ally, you actually believe that, don't you?" I can hear that it's a shock to him.

I finally look up at him. "Why wouldn't I?"

"Because you are most certainly **not** dumb, Ally."

"You're just saying that."

"No, I'm not, actually. For one, you are amazing on those bus driver math problems. You're one of the kids who gets the really harder ones correct."

I look up into his face with the bright sun behind him and blurt out, "But how come I can't read?" It's the first time I've ever asked the question out loud. I guess because I'm so desperate for an answer.

"Aw, Ally," he says, "this thing that makes school hard for you . . . I think you might have something called dyslexia. And it means that, although it's hard for you to read, it doesn't mean you're dumb." He laughs a little. "In fact, you, Ally Nickerson, are far from it. Your brain just figures things out differently than other people."

I'm different; he's got that right. But no way am I smart like he says. "You don't understand."

"Yeah, Ally, I think I do." Then he leans in. "And you know what? You're brave."

I so want to be brave, but I'm not.

. . .

"And you know something else? In some ways, you're a lot smarter than other kids. You can also do things they can't. For one, you're an amazing artist. Those drawings of yours! Wow, Ally. You've got talent there. What do you think about that?"

"I think it's like saying, 'I'm sorry you're going to die but at least people are going to bring you flowers.'"

(Continued)

(Continued)

He laughs really hard now. "See that? Seriously, Ally. Only smart people say things like that." His voice drops. "It's going to be okay, kiddo."

I have never hoped for something so much as this.

▶ **Let's look at dialogue and character thoughts again. How would you describe Ally now? What has she discovered about herself?**

▶ **Mr. Daniels is true to his word and he begins to work with Ally. It's hard work for her, but she makes progress. One day in class, Mr. Daniels starts to list numerous famous people like Albert Einstein, Leonardo da Vinci, Patricia Polacco, John Lennon, Walt Disney, Winston Churchill, and more and asks the students what they all have in common. It turns out to be dyslexia.**

[pp. 241–243]

But I'm still staring at the pictures of all those famous people and wondering if they felt like me when they were young? Did they feel stupid? Did they wonder what would become of them?

. . .

"This is a paperweight," he says. "It's a gift for you."

"For me?"

"Yes. Look." He points at each word as he reads them. "'*Never, never, never quit. Winston Churchill.*'"

I pick it up. It's heavy.

"I'm not giving it to you as a reminder, because I know that you will keep it. I've really gotten a sense lately of how hard you've had to work to learn what you have. And," he says, laughing, "you've fooled a lot of smart people. So, how smart does that make **you**?"

I swallow hard.

"I'm giving it to you because I want you to know that I've noticed. And that you're going to be okay, Ally." He leans forward a bit. "**Better** than okay, actually."

My head swims with all that's changed.

In school.

And in me.

▶ **This is not the end of the book, but Ally's thoughts signal a huge change. Why? How would you describe her now? Highlight where in this excerpt it helps to understand this.**

Note: Lynda Mullaly Hunt uses dialogue to reveal character and move the story along in these excerpts, but notice the powerful effect of Ally's internal monologue: "Seven schools in seven years and they're all the same. Whenever I do my best they tell me I don't try hard enough. Too messy. Careless spelling. Annoyed that the same word is spelled different ways on the same page. And the headaches. I always get headaches from looking at the brightness of dark letters on white pages for too long." When an author shows a character's response to what another has said—those fleeting, important emotional reactions—readers need to pay careful attention, as these moments offer important glimpses of character challenge and the seeds of character change and growth.

Notice Plot via Character Conflict/Change

PROMPTS FOR NOTICING PLOT VIA CHARACTER CONFLICT/CHANGE

- How does the main character behave at the beginning of the story? Why?

- How do characters react or respond to the setting?

- How do characters react or respond to other characters?

- How do characters react or respond to events?

- What is the main problem? What details in the text help you know this?

- What are the important events that lead up to the resolution?

- How do the characters respond or change as the plot develops over time?

 Available for download at
http://resources.corwin.com/evidencebasedwriting-fiction

Characters Respond to Challenges: In literature, characters face problems and respond or react to these challenges. The way they react moves the story along and adds to the event sequence. The problems can be internal conflicts, such as a character stuck in grief, fear, or more external challenges, such as troubled family or friendships.

Plot: The unfolding events through which the author reveals characters and their needs/wishes. Also known as storyline, and thought of as the arc of rising and falling dramatic action.

BEST THE TEST

Identifying character responses/reactions using literal and inferential thinking is a common task on tests. Make students aware that:

- The follow-up question requires selecting the line(s) in text that supports their answer, so practicing finding text evidence as they read will serve them well.

- The written assessment portion of the test often requires them to summarize plot, and they should include character response as a part of the summary.

- Give students practice with multiple-choice formats and highlighting supporting statements, then summarizing. Twice a month is ample. Remember: *Students should be reading independently and thinking about character and plot for sheer enjoyment!*

Lesson prep

- Choose a book to read aloud that has strong character change. (I use Eve Bunting's *Your Move* in this model lesson.) Familiarize yourself with the book, being ready to discuss with your students character description and events that cause reaction. (The first page of *Your Move* provides character description and sets up the problem.)

- Photocopy Think About Character (page 59) for each student to fill out as you read.

Introduce it

1. Distribute prompts to students and/or display them on a wall as an anchor chart.

2. Also create your own anchor chart with the prompts.

3. Tell students that today's purpose is to answer these questions: How do characters react and respond to the setting, events, or other characters? How does this cause them to change?

4. Read aloud *Your Move* (or some other book).

5. Stop at key points; have students jot on the response form and share thinking with peers.

6. Stop on the first page, instructing students to begin to fill in character description (e.g., told in first person, main character is 10, watches his little brother. What can they *infer* by the line "Tonight we're going out"?—*character is going to disobey the mother*).

7. Stop at important junctures and discuss where it fits on the chart. Use the prompts and the anchor chart to guide thinking. (Possible junctures are pp. 3, 9, 11, 15, 17, 22, 25, 27.)

8. When finished, ask: What is James like at the end of the book? How did he change?

9. **Write about reading:** Co-construct a three-paragraph response using the information from Think About Character. Photocopy these for each student to use as an example for future writing. *Co-constructing and providing students with solid examples is key to transfer to independence.*

10. Tell students they will be doing this same process, digging deeper into character.

For students who may need more structure or support, download the Character Response organizer at **http://resources.corwin.com/evidencebasedwriting-fiction**.

Dad, Jackie and Me by Myron Uhlberg

The Memory String by Eve Bunting

Mr. Peabody's Apples by Madonna

Mouse for Sale—how characters respond to challenges: https://youtu.be/UB3nKCNUBB4

HOW TO USE THE GRAB AND GO PAGES

- Distribute to students copies of Think About Character on page 59 and the text by R. J. Palacio on page 61.

- Either in small groups, with partners, or independently, students read and annotate the excerpts from "The Julian Chapter" to notice how characters change and why. (This book follows the novel *Wonder*, which is featured on page 131 in Section 4.)

- Have them fill out all but the paragraph-writing task on the Think About Character page.

- **On another day:** Have students complete the writing task. It's fine if they use the co-constructed three-paragraph response from the lesson to guide them.

- **Ongoing:** Provide students with additional practice with short pieces of text. Students who need more support can use the write-about-reading template, but many students may want to annotate in the margins and then go directly to paragraph-writing. Remember, though, to use paragraph writing judiciously. Use it as practice; too much can become overkill. We want students to love reading!

Your Move
by Eve Bunting

Purpose: How do characters respond to challenges? How do characters CHANGE?

Description:
- James – main character – narrator (first person)
- Isaac – 10 years old – older brother
- Dad – gone; little brother looks up to him

Events/Characters → Response

Beginning

- [Tonight I've not going out... have to meet... tonight] → Going to disobey → Nervous "Tonight I have to prove myself so I can be in their club too"

Middle

- [Tagging high above the freeway] → Scared My stomach felt going up I wish I could slink away / Does it writes 93bo I'm suddenly so cool
- [Take It game (stealing)] → Regretting decision "I'm not feeling too great about getting him into this"
- [Snakes – Gun] → Scared "The river felt my heart slide around the way its sliding now." / Run Isaac falls & scrapes knees James lies to Mom

ENDING

- [Kris brings Lakers cap and talks about being in gang / club cap?] → Gives it back Isaac gives it back too / They don't want to be part of the gang / Its the big brother role model for Isaac

---

—James

The main character is James. He is also the narrator (the story is first person). James is ten years old and the big brother to Isaac (1). Their dad is gone and their mother works at night. At the beginning James disobeys his mother and sneaks out to meet his friends. He says, "Tonight I have to prove myself so I can be in their club, too." He wants to fit in.

James reacted to two big events in the story. The first was when he was told to "tag" high above the freeway. He was scared and "wished I could slink away," but he did it and even though Isaac was scared, James felt cool. The second thing that happened was Kris talks about the "Take It" game which is stealing and then the Snakes come and shoot their gun. James regrets the decision to bring Isaac ("I'm not feeling too great about getting him into this") and scared when the gun shows up. The boys run, Isaac falls and scrapes his knees but they make it home. James lies to his mother about how Isaac got hurt.

James changes at the end of the book when Kris comes to give James and Isaac Lakers caps and to tell them they're in the club. James gives it back, and Isaac does too. Isaac copies him. They don't want to be in the club. James learned/changed from the events that happened. I think he wants to be a good big brother and role model for Isaac. I think he realized how bad the club was.

Think About Character

Name(s): _____

Title: _____

Main Character: _____

1. Jot down descriptive words and examples to help you write a description of the character.

_____

_____

_____

_____

2. How did the character react and respond to setting, events, or other characters? Jot down notes and evidence. How does this help you understand character?

Setting	Events	Characters

3. What was the character like at the end of the story? Did he or she change? Give examples from the text.

_____

_____

_____

_____

(Continued)

(Continued)

Directions:

Use your notes to write three paragraphs about the character over the course of the text. Each paragraph corresponds to the number on the organizer.

Paragraph 1
Character Description (support reasoning)
Give at least three examples.

Paragraph 2
Explain at least two examples of how the character reacted or responded to setting, events, or characters. Use examples from the text. Explain why this was important and how it helped to understand the character better.

Paragraph 3
Describe what the character was like at the end of the book. Did the character change? You may add your opinion in this section and write about how you feel about the character and your thoughts.

Available for download at **http://resources.corwin.com/evidencebasedwriting-fiction**

EXCERPTS TO WRITE ABOUT

"The Julian Chapter"

From *Auggie and Me: Three Wonder Stories*

by R. J. Palacio

▶ In *Wonder*, Julian is the major protagonist, although the story is never told from his point of view. He bullies the main character, Auggie, unmercifully and never apologizes, nor feels remorse. Ultimately he is punished for his behavior, but still doesn't own it; instead he blames others. In "The Julian Chapter" we finally get his point of view, which begins like this:

Beginning [p. 1]

Okay, okay, okay.

I know, I know, I know.

I haven't been nice to August Pullman!

Big deal. It's not the end of the world, people! Let's stop with the drama, okay? There's a whole big world out there, and not everyone is nice to everyone else. That's just the way it is. So, can you please get over it? I think it's time to move on and get on with your life, don't you?

Jeez!

I don't get it. I really don't. One minute, I'm like, the most popular kid in the fifth grade. And the next minute, I'm like, I don't know. Whatever. This bites. This whole year bites! I wish Auggie Pullman had never come to Beecher Prep in the first place! I wish he had kept his creepy little face hidden away like in *The Phantom of the Opera* or something. Put a mask on, Auggie! Get your face out of my face, please. Everything would be a lot easier if you would just disappear.

At least for me. I'm not saying it's a picnic for him, either, by the way. I know it can't be easy for him to look in the mirror every day, or walk down the street. But that's not my problem. My problem is that everything's different since he's been coming to my school. The kids are different. I'm different. And it sucks big time.

▶ As you read this, what are you thinking of Julian? How would you describe him? With one color, highlight the text that gives you information about him. Jot character traits to match what you've underlined. With a second color, highlight where Julian is reacting to characters and events and jot your thinking.

▶ When Julian receives his punishment, what bothers the adults most is his lack of *remorse*. That word shows up repeatedly in this short story. He spends the summer in France with his Grandmere who recounts the story of the cripple Tourteau who saved her from the Nazis but ultimately lost his life. She tells the story because Tourteau had been tormented for his deformity and it reminded her of Auggie. Julian also finds out that Tourteau's real name was Julian. Grandmere's story touches him and he continues to ask questions.

Middle [pp. 82–84]

But when I heard you talking about that little boy in your school, I could not help but think of Tourteau, of how afraid I had been of him, of how badly we had treated him because of his deformity.

(Continued)

(Continued)

. . .

When she said that, I don't know, something just really broke inside of me. Completely unexpected. I looked down and, all of a sudden, I started to cry. And when I say I started to cry, I don't mean a few tears rolling down my cheeks—I mean like, full-scale, snot-filled crying.

"Julian," she said softly.

I shook my head and covered my face with my hands.

"I was terrible, Grandmere," I whispered. "I was so mean to Auggie. I'm so sorry, Grandmere!"

"Julian," she said again, "Look at me."

"No!"

"Look at me, *mon cher*." She took my face in her hands and forced me to look at her. I felt so embarrassed. I really couldn't look her in the eyes. Suddenly, that word that Mr. Tushman had used, that word that everyone kept trying to force on me, came to me like a shout. REMORSE!

Yeah, there it was. The word in all its glory.

REMORSE. I was shaking with remorse. I was crying with remorse.

"Julian," said Grandmere. "We all make mistakes, *mon cher*."

"No, you don't understand!" I answered. "It wasn't just one mistake. I *was* those kids who were mean to Tourteau. . . . I was the bully, Grandmere. It was me!"

She nodded.

"I called him a freak. I laughed behind his back. I *left mean notes*!" I screamed. "Mom kept making excuses for why I did that stuff . . . but there wasn't any excuse. I just did it! And I don't even know why. I don't even know.

. . .

"But the good thing about life, Julian," she continued, "is that we can fix our mistakes sometimes. We learn from them. We get better. . . . One mistake does not define you, Julian."

▶ **Why is this an important passage for defining Julian's character? Does he change? Why? Highlight and annotate key parts. How does dialogue help you understand his reaction?**

▶ **After this, Julian reaches out to his teachers to begin to explain a bit. He apologizes to Auggie. He understands remorse and asks his Grandmere if Tourteau would forgive him. And he stops his mother from pursuing a lawsuit against the school. He takes the high road—and takes ownership. When he returns home, there is a message on the answering machine from Auggie accepting the apology and wishing Julian well in his new school. Julian wasn't expecting that.**

(Continued)

(Continued)

End [pp. 95–96]

"Are you going to call him back?" asked Dad.

I shook my head. "Nah," I answered. "I'm too chicken."

Dad walked over to me and put his hand on my shoulder.

"I think you've proven that you're anything *but* chicken," he said. "I'm proud of you, Julian. Very proud of you." He leaned over and hugged me. *"Tu marches toujours le front haut*."*

I smiled. "I hope so, Dad."

I hope so.

*You always walk with your head high.

▶ **How would you describe Julian now? How does dialogue affect character? How did Julian change from the beginning of this story to the end and why?**

Note: Chapters in Palacio's novel are told from various characters' points of view. Here, we see the world through the eyes of a boy who bullied Auggie, whose face is deformed.

The novelist's heavy use of dialogue in many regards expresses her theme: that despite hardships, when we have close connections with family and friends, we have the energy to keep our spirits up. Have your students consider the grandmother's words: "'But the good thing about life, Julian,' she continued, 'is that we can fix our mistakes sometimes. We learn from them. We get better. . . . One mistake does not define you, Julian.'" This is an example of how an author can embed her message/ beliefs in the words of a character.

Notice How Character Drives Plot

BEST THE TEST

Plot shows up on tests in different forms. Students may address it via multiple choice or writing about the main problem and solution. As students progress through the grades, text sophistication increases, and thus students need to be able to identify multiple plots. More tips:

- Teach students to compare/contrast plots and character reactions within a text and between two texts.

- Students need to understand the difference between *plot* (what happens, including the problem/solution) and *theme* (the central idea or message).

- Summarizing requires identifying the most important events, and to do so students need to be adept at communicating how events relate to characters' problems.

LESSON PREP

- Revisit a picture book or short story to teach plot and the important elements that are included when you write about plot (for example, *Your Move* or *Thank You, Mr. Falker*).

- Have different colored sticky note "flags" available to placehold different elements.

- Create a Story Map anchor chart with terms defined.

- Create a blank Story Map anchor chart (see example on page 68).

INTRODUCE IT

1. Revisit a book that students have already read, and share that they will focus on the connections between characters and plot.

2. Review the defined Story Map chart and discuss the terms. Label one colored sticky note "Exposition," use another color for "Climax," another color "Resolution," and place numbers on the remaining sticky

notes of another color. Place these on the blank chart where they might belong. (Put the numbered flags on "rising action" and on the higher numbers on "falling action.")

3. Read the book, stopping to discuss and placing the sticky notes where they belong. Using sticky notes allows for repositioning as thinking changes.

4. Discuss that plot includes the *most important* events, and remove and move numbered flags. Make sure students flag events that tie to plot or to character.

5. When satisfied with the location of the flags, discuss whether students have captured the chronology and important points.

For plot maps for Grades 6–8, go to the companion website at **http://resources.corwin.com/evidencebasedwriting-fiction**.

Because of Winn-Dixie by Kate DiCamillo

Esperanza Rising by Pam Munoz Ryan

Hatchet by Gary Paulsen

Runaway—plot versus theme: https://youtu.be/lOReXHOSnvw

WRITE-ABOUT-READING TEMPLATE

GRAB & GO

Plot Chart

Name: _____ Date: _____
Title: _____

Setting:

Main Character:

Problem:

Events:

1.

2.

3.

Climax:

Conclusion/Resolution:

WRITE-ABOUT-READING TEMPLATE

GRAB & GO

Plot Map

Name: _____ Date: _____
Title: _____

Climax

Plot

Rising Actions (main events)

Falling Action

Conflict

Resolution

Exposition

Protagonist vs. Antagonist vs.

Setting

Characters

Theme

HOW TO USE THE GRAB AND GO PAGES

- Distribute to students copies of Story Map on page 68 and Write About Character and Plot on page 69.

- Using a picture book or a short story of their choice, students repeat the process outlined in the lesson above, placing sticky notes on their story map pages as they read. (Students can work in groups if that is easier.)

- After they finish a book and fill out a Story Map, students fill out the Write About Character and Plot page.

- **Ongoing:** Move from working in short texts to using the Story Map with a chapter book. Encourage students to use this work to support their writing literary essays.

- In time, have students design their own visual maps to capture the rising and falling action throughout a story. Have students add to their charts how characters respond or change as the plot develops over time. Introduce different, more sophisticated Plot Maps as students progress through the grades.

- **A word of caution:** Let students read for the joy of reading and to escape into books! Don't make them "work over" every book they read, otherwise reading becomes a chore to be avoided!

SAMPLES TO SHARE WITH STUDENTS

Title: Keep A Lid On It, Pandora

Author: Kate Mcmullan

Characters:

Hades
Zeus
Pandora
Prometheus
Epi

Prometheus and Epi make guys and animals out of clay/magic clay that makes it all come alive. They also gave them gifts.

Zeus Imbe tricked Prometheus behind this hunt

Then some guys and god's behind Pandora got tricked and the world stay alive

Prometheus and Epi make guys that try can't be good

Fire & smartness so the Pandora starts to spit out

Then Pandora have and tripets again.

Climax!

Then Zeus and Hades make a bet that Pandora wont open this box and Zeus ends up cheating.

Zeus ended up tricking Pandora into opening the box, by discising it as a first-add-kit and pretending to be hurt.

And everyone started crying when the box was opned, because all the bad things in the world came out, so life wasn't perfect.

Resolution:

The resolution was nobody won the bet of $10,000 on Pandora, all because Zeus cheated. And Hades was playing pretty fair.

Settings:

Mount Olympus,
The Underworld,
Gug town and
the rocky
Caucasus Moun-
tains.

POV:

1st person
↓
Hades is
telling it.

Theme:

Don't let
your curiousity
get the best
of you, is
the theme.

Conflict:

The conflict of the story is that Zeus and Hades made a bet on what Pandora was going to do and when Hades was winning Zeus cheated, and it got crazy.

Story Map

Name: _____

Title: _____

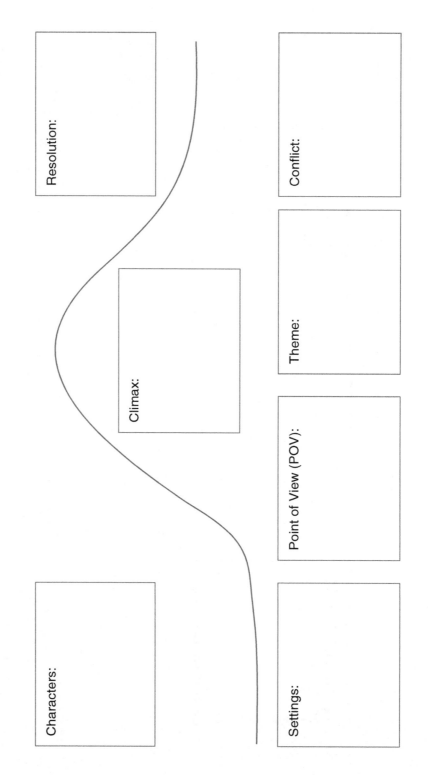

Characters:

Resolution:

Climax:

Settings:

Point of View (POV):

Theme:

Conflict:

Available for download at **http://resources.corwin.com/evidencebasedwriting-fiction**

Write About Character and Plot

For Grades 3–6

Task

- Write an essay reflecting on the main character in your book.

- Describe the character in detail, using evidence from the text (at least two examples).

- Explain how the character reacted to an event or to another character.

- How did that help you understand the character?

- How did the character change from the beginning of the book to the end?

- Use evidence from the text to explain *why* that change occurred.

- In this essay, also reflect on your feelings about the character and why you feel that way.

For Grade 6

Task

- Describe how the plot of the story unfolds.

- What are the key episodes and why?

- Include how the main character responds or changes.

- How is the story resolved, and how has the character changed?

Develop Theories About Characters

Character Theory: To create a theory about a character, the reader *analyzes* (careful and close examination, typically for the purposes of explanation and interpretation). Good readers don't hold *conclusions* about characters so much as they continually revise first assumptions based on new details the author provides as the story unfolds. By story's end, a reader has synthesized information and in essence tries to reach a conclusion about a character(s).

PROMPTS FOR DEVELOPING THEORIES ABOUT CHARACTERS

- How does the narrator's point of view influence understanding of the character?
- What do the character's relationships with others suggest about the character?
- What do the character's relationships with objects suggest about the character?
- How does the character's reactions help to define her or him?
- Why does the character's behavior change from the beginning of the story to the end? What has she or he learned?
- Which events or specific lines of dialogue most affect the story? (Grades 6–8)
- How do these events or specific lines affect the story the most? (Grades 6–8)
- What does this event or dialogue reveal about the character? (Grades 6–8)

 Available for download at
http://resources.corwin.com/evidencebasedwriting-fiction

BEST THE TEST

At the risk of sounding flippant, "provide evidence" is to tests what "eat six servings of fruits and vegetables" is to nutrition! In other words, there is nothing wrong with such advice, but it will never stick if we don't allow our students plenty of choice daily—plenty of opportunities for students to just go into the reading zone (Atwell, 2007), getting lost in their books without caring one whit about evidence. So my counterintuitive advice:

- Help students read well by allowing them to read lots.
- When students have a purpose, task, and *choice,* reading for evidence becomes authentic.
- Allow time every day for meaningful literacy conversations among peers, as this deepens comprehension and engagement.

LESSON PREP

- Choose a book with strong characters and plot. (I use Jacqueline Woodson's *The Other Side* for this model lesson.) Use sticky notes to mark your thinking *ahead of time* about character traits and your theory. For example: On p. 2, the fence is important because it separates the white family from the black family; main character is black. On p. 4, the fence separates two girls. On p. 5, the character doesn't always follow what her friends say; she might have let the white girl play. Continue this way until p. 13. Discuss the line "I felt brave that day. I felt free." You might have a theory like "I think the main character wants to follow her mother's rules, but she wants to be friends with the girl across the fence and she doesn't care about the fence. I think she thinks finding a friend is more important."

- Have chart paper on hand to hold thinking.

INTRODUCE IT

1. Distribute prompts to students and/or display them on the wall as an anchor chart.

2. Also create your own anchor chart with the prompts.

3. Ask and discuss: What is a theory?

4. Think aloud as you read from the pages you've flagged. When you get to the page where you've written your theory, ask these questions before you share your thinking: Why do you think the character acts the way she does? What motivates her? How can I group my sticky notes to help me come up with a theory? Share your theory and write it at the top of the chart paper. Then divide the rest of the chart into two columns and label one column "Evidence" and the other "How This Supports My Thinking."

5. Model by going back through the first sticky notes on character, adding the ones to the chart that support the theory, and throwing away the others.

6. Tell students that now as you read your purpose will be to find evidence that confirms your theory or makes you revise your theory.

7. Finish reading the book, adding sticky notes to the chart and revising if needed.

8. Fill in the column "How This Supports My Thinking."

9. **Write about reading:** Co-construct a response that addresses the theory, the evidence, and how that supports the theory. Do this on chart paper or type it and photocopy for students to have as an example.

10. Tell students they will be doing this same process you are now modeling to create their own theories about characters in the books they're reading.

To learn more about Jacqueline Woodson: http://www.jacquelinewoodson.com

This website is more appropriate for older students: http://www.npr.org/sections/codeswitch/2014/12/10/369736205/jacqueline-woodson-on-growing-up-coming-out-and-saying-hi-to-strangers

Pink and Say by Patricia Polacco

The Butterfly by Patricia Polacco

Tom, Babette, and Simon: Three Tales of Transformation by Avi

A couple of interviews with Jacqueline Woodson:

- http://www.readingrockets.org/books/interviews/woodson

- https://youtu.be/IqMkiFSkutY

HOW TO USE THE GRAB AND GO PAGES

- Distribute to students copies of Create a Theory About a Character on page 73. If you are comparing two characters use Compare/Contrast Characters on page 74.

- Have students read and annotate a picture book or short story on their own, using the same process you just modeled.

- Students record their thinking on sticky notes and follow the write-about-reading template.

- When finished, students share their organizers with partners or in small groups. They can add to or revise their thinking as they discuss.

- When they are satisfied with their theory and evidence, students write a short response using the co-constructed piece as a model.

- **On another day:** Have students go through the process again with another book. They can then use the reproducible to compare and contrast characters across books.

- **Ongoing:** Use the compare/contrast chart for any literary elements as students read a variety of books for a variety of purposes.

SAMPLE TO SHARE WITH STUDENTS

Theory: an idea or set of ideas that is intended to explain facts or events (Merriam Webster)

Purpose: Develop a Theory about a character. Find the evidence.

The Other Side
by Jacqueline Woodson

My theory: I think the main character (narrator) wants to follow her mom's rules, but she wants to be friends across the fence even more. She thinks having a friend is more important than a fence.

Evidence	How this supports my thinking
And Mama said, "Don't climb over that fence when you play." It isn't safe. p.2 · Why? p.8 "Because that's the way things have always been." - Mama · I see you made a new friend. - Mama p.24	Mama doesn't think it's safe. They're black and across the fence they're white
She acted if she could play. I don't know what I would have said maybe no. p.3 · She let herself get all wet and acted like she didn't care p.9 · But every time it rained I looked for that girl. And I always found her. Somewhere near the fence p.12 · I felt brave that day. I felt free p.14	Wants to be friends Annie looks like she's fun
And then I all smiled. It's nice up on this fence. You can see all over. A fence like this was made for sitting on. · Mama never said nothing about sitting on it p.19 · That summer me and Annie sat on that fence and watched the whole world around. · Someday somebody's going to come along and knock this old fence down. p.29	The girls make friends and figure out how to be together and not disobey their parents ✳ Important!

Create a Theory About Character

Name(s): _____

Title: _____

Main Character: _____

Directions:

- Read the beginning of the book and use sticky notes to hold your thinking about character traits. Use the prompts that help readers create theories about characters to guide you. Make sure to jot the page number on your sticky notes.

- When you think you have a theory about your character, stop and go back through your sticky notes. (You should have a theory before you're halfway through the book.) Group the ones that support your theory; if you have enough evidence, write your theory on the organizer. Put your sticky notes in the column and write how they support your thinking.

- Read the rest of the book with the purpose of proving your theory or revising your theory. Continue to mark your thinking on sticky notes.

- When you finish, add sticky notes with the best evidence to your chart and finish filling it out.

My theory about my character is:	
Support or Evidence	
Sticky Notes With Jots (Evidence)	**How This Supports My Thinking**

Compare/Contrast Characters

Name(s): _____

Title: _____

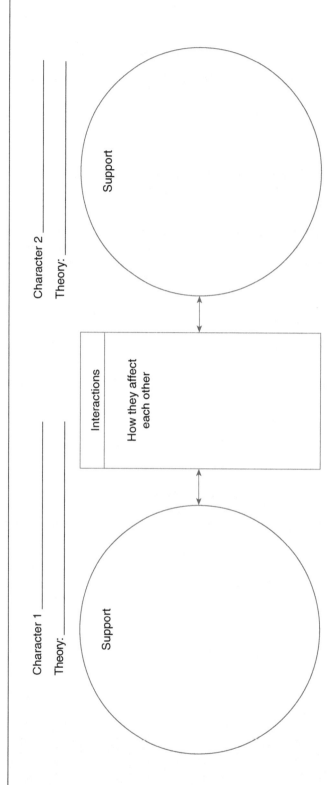

Character 1 _____

Theory: _____

Character 2 _____

Theory: _____

Support

Support

Interactions

How they affect each other

Write about reading:

- How are the characters similar?
- How are the characters different?
- How did events in the text influence them?

Analyze Character

BEST THE TEST

As students progress through the intermediate grades and middle school, they must infer, analyze, and demonstrate understanding of ever more sophisticated texts. You can prepare students for this increased challenge by:

- Giving written tasks like the one on page 78, as this task reflects aspects of the writing portion of standardized tests. (Often on exams students are asked to continue the storyline by adding a chapter.)

- Ensuring students can handle longer writing in response to reading.

- Giving ample practice with compare and contrast. Even with shared books, make authentic comparing and contrasting a part of discussion.

LESSON PREP

- Read a full-length novel so you know it well. (I use *Here Where the Sunbeams Are Green* by Helen Phillips in this lesson.) You can also use this as a read-aloud and to model your thinking. This novel lends itself to all literary elements and is always a class favorite. Or just have students work with the excerpts included here.

- Photocopy the Character Essay: Task/Assessment Options page and the story excerpts by Helen Phillips on page 78.

INTRODUCE IT

1. Model thinking about creating a theory about characters with a read-aloud book, and show how to hold thinking across a chapter book. Use two different colored sticky notes—one color for main character and the other color for other literary elements. Demonstrate how to be judicial with sticky notes. (More is not necessarily better!)

2. Or use the story excerpts on pages 79–81 with important scenes that help understand character.

3. Guide the students through the text and how it shows character development.

4. Refer to the anchor chart from the warm-up lesson on page 70.

See **http://resources.corwin.com/ evidencebasedwriting-fiction** for more excerpts from *Here Where the Sunbeams Are Green* for setting.

While I've used *Here Where the Sunbeams Are Green* in this chapter for literary elements, it is also a fantastic chapter book for working with theme. Using books for multiple purposes (revisiting them) is always good practice!

Number the Stars by Lois Lowry

Flying Solo by Ralph Fletcher

Crenshaw by Katherine Applegate

The Tiger Rising by Kate DiCamillo

Liar and Spy by Rebecca Stead

Trailer for *Here Where the Sunbeams Are Green*: https://youtu.be/P9sP5AJsnpg

HOW TO USE THE GRAB AND GO PAGES

- Distribute to students copies of Character Essay: Task/Assessment Options on page 78.

  - **Option 1:** Use as a teacher-guided lesson. Have students use the handout and the story excerpts to notice, annotate, and create a theory about characters from *Here Where the Sunbeams Are Green*. (Possible theories: Mad loves her family and even though she's a bit jealous of Roo she will do anything for her. Or Mad is different from Roo. Roo is outgoing and not scared; Mad likes to read, write poetry, and is scared of lots of stuff.) *Optional: Or respond to how two characters interact and how that creates theory.*

  - **Option 2:** Use these excerpts to help you work through a shared reading of the entire novel, *stopping at these points in particular* to discuss aspects of character and create a theory.

- Model how in the initial chapters you gather clues about character traits and then group them to create a theory. From that point on you read with the purpose of finding evidence to prove or disprove the theory.

- Model how you keep sticky notes that support the theory in your reader's notebook (with page numbers) and throw away sticky notes that are no longer needed.

- As you model your strategies, students transfer these skills to their own independent reading, supported by the prompts on page 70, sticky notes, and reading journals.

- Allow time for students to discuss their thinking with partners or in small groups.

- Assign one of the tasks from the handout that fit your grade level and student needs, and give students multiple days to complete the writing when they finish the book.

- **Ongoing:** Create your own excerpts page or invite students to create excerpts pages (this can also be used as an assessment) from their own books. That is truly an authentic assessment!

Hatchet

Brian

My theory Brian is that he with keep feeling guilty until he gets to tell his mom or dad or really anyone what he saw that caused the divorce. This is probably why he keep repeting things like, divorce, the secret, fight, split, and so on.
        This gonna keep repeting those words.

proofi

• keeps repeting those words, the secret...

• No one knows what he saw, feels guilty because didn't tell anyone and he doesn't want to keep a secret himself.
    ↓
    feels   • He keeps bringing it
    guilty   up in the book.
    for
    not
    telling

Character Essay: Task/Assessment Options

Name: _____   Date: _____

Title: _____

Task

As you read through your assigned book, pay particular attention to *character*. As we get farther into books, we will be discussing how readers create *theories* about a character and then reading to prove or disprove that theory. As you read, your thinking may change, but when you finish your book, you will write an essay analyzing character. In this essay you will state your theory about why your character acted the way he or she did and how he or she changed throughout the story. You will need to support your theory with at least three examples from the text.

Task

Part 1

Reflect on the main character in the book. Write a detailed description of the character using examples from the text. Then analyze how the character changed from the beginning of the book to the end and *why*. Use at least three examples from the book to support this.

Part 2

Write another chapter to the book that extends the story.

Task

Lessons learned by a character in one book can be compared to other characters in other books (think Polacco and Hunt).

How does understanding the character in one book help us grow theories about new characters?

For Grades 7–8

Task

Analyze how characters interact and the conflicts that occur. What do these conflicts reflect about the characters? How does this affect the plot?

What evidence do you have from the text to support your claim? Explain how the evidence supports your claim.

Available for download at **http://resources.corwin.com/evidencebasedwriting-fiction**

EXCERPTS TO WRITE ABOUT

Here Where the Sunbeams Are Green

by Helen Phillips

▶ Mad and Roo are sisters who get wrapped up in a mystery set in a Central American country. Their father, Dr. Wade, a famous ornithologist, has been working for La Lava, an exclusive "green" spa at the foot of a volcano. However, he hasn't come home to Denver for months, so the girls and their mother go to see him. And that's when things get even stranger. We meet Mad as their plane is going to land.

[p. 1]

So here we are in this shaky little airplane high above the jungle, which is kind of (very) scary. On our first flight Roo got the window seat the whole five hours, so she insisted that I get it for the second flight, which is pretty thoughtful for someone who's only nine-almost-ten. But I really should've let her have the window seat this time too. Even though I'm three years older than my sister, she's the brave one who loves flying and other dangerous things. Plus I've been a bit more freaked out in general lately, ever since The Weirdness began. The amazing view is basically wasted on me—the only way I can get through the wobbly ride is by pressing my forehead hard against the window, trying to pretend the jungle below is a huge green trampoline and even if we fell out of the sky we'd be totally fine.

▶ Who is telling the story and how does that affect your thinking? From this paragraph, what clues do you have about Mad? Highlight sections of the text that support your thinking and jot character traits.

▶ As you read through the following excerpts, add traits in the margins. Highlight the evidence and think about how you know—through thoughts, feelings, words, or actions.

[pp. 8–9]

I used to be a tiny bit jealous of Roo and Dad's code thing. . . . I'm not really into that kind of thing. I'd rather just read, you know, books with stories. Like the ones Mom always brings home from her job at the library. But Dad and Roo had their code thing . . . but then it got more and more complicated and I lost track of it, and I had a small feeling of, Hey, what about me?

[p. 9]

I pull out my poetry notebook, which I've been using a ton ever since I made the New Year's resolution to write a poem a day.

[p. 10]

"Do you think Dad is coming up with something special for us when he sees us?"

Suddenly there's a huge lump in my throat. I can hardly wait to see him. I can't believe it's been seven whole months.

"Something special?" I say. "What kind of thing?"

"Well"—Roo pauses, thinking—"like, a song he made up just for us. Or a cake with our names on it."

Sometimes I feel so much older than Roo.

(Continued)

(Continued)

"I have no idea," I snap at her. "He's probably doing actual *work* right now."

I don't want Roo to know that my heart's swelling with excitement. It scares me to be this excited about seeing Dad. It makes me feel superstitious, like things might go extra wrong the more excited I am. I know if Dad were here, he'd tell me to take a deep breath. Slow and steady wins the race, Madpie. Slow and steady.

[p. 23]

"Don't you wish this was our own private pool?" I said to Roo earlier.

"Kind of," Roo said, but I could tell she didn't. She likes other people. Wherever she goes, Roo always has oodles of friends. Sometimes I've been jealous of her, but mostly I just admire her for being that way.

[p. 55]

Um, *hello*, I'll be thirteen in September—I can take care of me and Roo, obviously! But I don't say anything out loud. We've already had this fight a bunch of times. I am *so* sick of babysitters. Mom sometimes tries to call them "companions," as though that'll trick me into not realizing what they are.

▶ **Now it's time to come up with a theory about Mad. Look back through your jots and the traits you've listed. Look for similarities—how you might group them. Cross off any traits that don't fit. From the ones that remain, think of a theory about Mad (refer to our anchor chart on questions and prompts that help create theories), and write it as a statement here:**

_____

_____

_____

_____

▶ **As you read the next excerpts, look for evidence that supports your theory and highlight it. If you find evidence that *disproves* your theory, go back and revise! Continue to add your jots about your thinking.**

[pp. 72–73]

"Roo—she's gone, she's missing, where is she!" I panic.

. . .

We can't walk hand in hand on the narrow path, so Kyle lets go of me. I immediately start to feel more freaked out, if that's possible, more worried about Roo than I've ever been (and I've worried about Roo *a lot* in my lifetime). For some reason, though, I don't think I should keep calling her name. There's a hush over this part of the jungle, the animal sounds somehow muted here, a kind of quiet that seems as though it might have ears. I have this weird feeling that by saying Roo's name I might put her in extra danger. Instead, we just creep down the path, vines and leaves smacking my legs and face.

[p. 144]

"We have to do this, Mad," he murmurs.

(Continued)

(Continued)

"I know," I murmur back. Because I do know. They have to do it. Roo and Kyle. They're the ones who can do great things. They're the ones with powers. It's not like I haven't known all along that they can do things I can't. That they know things I don't. "You do."

"*We* do," Kyle corrects me. "We need you too."

[pp. 165–166]

"WE HAVE TO DO THIS!" Roo shrieks at me. "IT'S IN OUR BLOOD."

In our blood? I get an image of a flock of miniature birds flying through my veins.

"IN OUR BLOOD?" I echo, gazing at the Lava Throat.

And right then, before I've even finished saying *blood*, something happens inside me. Something changes, something clicks, and suddenly I'm not doubtful anymore. I don't know exactly what's going on, but I know that it's somehow coming from seeing the photo of the bird. I feel strong. Like Kyle. Like Roo. The strength rushes through me, pounding in my head and feet. Yes. We have our Mission. Dad always said everyone needs a mission in life. And he's right. It's good to know what you need to do and then go and do it. And yes, I'll admit it: I've always dreamed of being the heroine of a story like this one.

▶ **From these last excerpts, has your theory changed? Has Mad changed—and does that confirm your theory? Write a response stating your theory and giving three examples that support it.**

Note: What's impressive about this novel is that it will appeal to those students who love an adventure story, and yet as is evident in these excerpts, the author takes care to develop two sisters who have distinct characters that change over time. One craft element my students and I like to notice in the excerpts on these pages—and throughout the novel—is the way the author helps us learn about personality traits via the narrator's own responses to dialogue: "'Don't you wish this was our own private pool?' I said to Roo earlier. 'Kind of,' Roo said, but I could tell she didn't. She likes other people. Wherever she goes, Roo always has oodles of friends. Sometimes I've been jealous of her, but mostly I just admire her for being that way."

In the rest of the novel and in any novels your students read, have them pay attention to the language that is spliced in between what is spoken for clues to how a protagonist is thinking and feeling.

SECTION 3

Themes

Romeo loves Juliet, Dorothy dreams of Oz, Rob and Sistine care for a caged tiger—those are the literal topics of these famous works, but the themes are a different story! Love, fate, there's no place like home, trust, and embrace life despite past hurts are the big-idea themes that bubble up from the story's surface. That's what we need our students to discover each and every time they read.

In this section, I share lessons and practice pages that help students tease out the difference between topic and theme. The key skill? Inferring. Students have to combine clues in the text with their own background knowledge, in a sense weaving their inferences to eventually see the whole cloth pattern: the theme.

When I talk to students about themes, I find it's helpful to talk about theme versus plot. I explain that the plot is simply what happens in the narrative. "The themes represent the bigger ideas of the story. The plot carries those ideas along" (Harvey & Goudvis, 2007, p. 143). The theme is also the message. Harvey and Goudvis (2007) define it well: "Themes are the underlying ideas, morals, and lessons that give the story its texture, depth, and meaning. The themes are rarely explicitly stated in the story. We infer themes [and we] feel it in our gut" (p. 143).

In testing situations, however, gut feelings are only half the battle. Students must support their thinking about theme with specific evidence or lines from the text. So if we can support this in authentic ways, we are teaching reading and writing *and* savvy test taking.

I encourage you to work on reading for theme in advance of these text-based writing lessons. What could that look like? An easy way to "frontload" theme is to make it a part of discussions after you finish a shared text. Create a classroom chart of themes from the books read throughout the year. Additionally, students can jot what they think the theme is on sticky notes, and you can use these as "exit slips." I have a "Parking Lot" poster where students place their exit slips. Jotting builds stamina for more in-depth evidence-based writing about theme.

You'll see a lot of *why* and *how* questions in the pages ahead. Why did you decide on that theme? Why do you think that's the central message? Can you tell me why you think that, using information from the text? How did the author help you come to that conclusion? By posing these questions, we put the *students* in the driver's seat of doing the thinking and finding evidence from the text. Once they know how to answer these questions, they can write about theme and their *thinking* using evidence from the text to support it.

Watch Leslie Teach!

Video 3: **Watch how Leslie guides students to talk as a way into writing about theme, using a popular novel.**

Go to **http://resources.corwin.com/evidencebasedwriting-fiction** to see the lessons and guided practice in action.

Examples of student thinking on stickies on our class "Parking Lot"

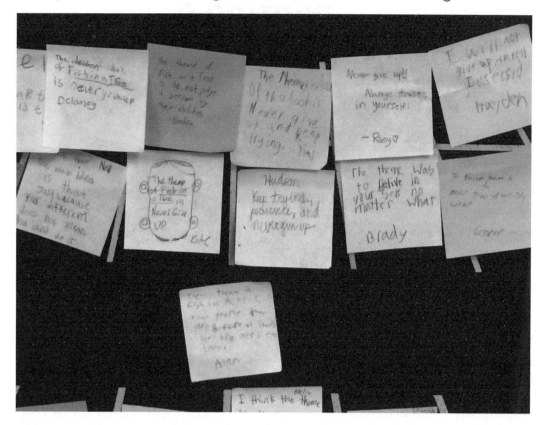

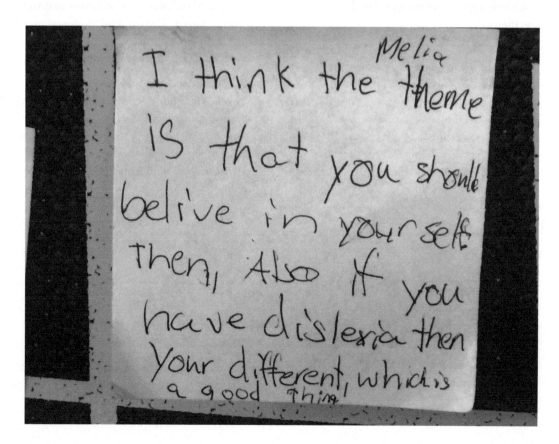

Determine Theme in Story

PROMPTS FOR DETERMINING THEME IN STORY

- Are there words or pictures that repeat?

- Does the author keep mentioning a particular object?

- Does something unexpected happen?

- Is there a moment of crisis for the main character?

- Does the main character ask questions that reveal his or her inner struggle?

- Does the character reflect on important memories?

- What does the last page say?

 Available for download at
http://resources.corwin.com/evidencebasedwriting-fiction

Theme: The central message of a story. May also be a lesson or a moral. It's what the author wants you to come away with in regard to an idea about life or human nature.

BEST THE TEST

Make discussing theme a natural part of your day. Use the books you share with your students or read aloud as a way to incorporate theme into the daily weave of your classroom. Fables, folktales, myths, and legends are used on tests, so give students exposure to and practice with these text types. I tend to practice at least once a month, just to give you a ballpark. More tips:

- Give students practice with multiple-choice formats, highlighting sentences from the text and explaining thinking in writing. Again, at least twice a month is beneficial.

- As a class, over time, do a mix of interactive whiteboard group work and individual practice during which students read, highlight, and annotate on photocopies. This should be a regular activity, not necessarily a test practice activity.

LESSON PREP

- Choose a book rich with theme (such as Eve Bunting's *Fly Away Home*). Place three to five sticky notes on pages that contain language that especially hints at theme (e.g., p. 6, "Dad and I try not to be noticed" suggests to me that these two characters want to be almost invisible so they won't be caught. Imagine what it would be like to go through life not being noticed.).

- Photocopy What's the Theme? (page 89) and "The Mighty" (page 90).

INTRODUCE IT

1. Distribute prompts to students and/or display them on the wall as an anchor chart.

2. Also create your own anchor chart with the prompts.

3. Read aloud *Fly Away Home* (or some other book in which theme is evident).

4. Think aloud as you read the pages you've flagged, being sure to address the prompts for theme listed on the anchor chart. (Possible junctures are pp. 8, 12, 15, 22, 30, which highlight a repeating line or focus of *not being noticed*.) Be explicit as you think aloud.

5. In this book, an important part for discerning theme is page 16, with the symbol of the bird and the title: "'Fly, bird,' I whispered, 'Fly away home!'" Let the students do the noticing. If they miss this the first time, skim or reread and discuss. The bird also is on the last page, which is an additional hint to theme.

6. When you finish the book, ask: What are some possible themes? (Personal freedom, the importance of home and belonging, friendship, family and working together can overcome long odds and adversity.) How do you know? What is in the text to help you?

7. Model how you revisit your sticky notes and choose and write on three sticky notes that represent the strongest evidence of theme. Then transfer the sticky notes to the write-about-reading template.

8. Write about reading: Co-construct a short response on the write-about-reading template stating the theme and *why* you think this, using the evidence from the text. If possible, include or cite more than one example. Make sure to state the theme in a sentence! *This is key to modeling the transfer from reading about theme to writing about theme.*

9. Tell students they will be doing this same process you are now modeling, answering the question: What was the theme and what details in the text helped you determine that?

For students who may need more structure and support, download the Theme Summarizer at **http://resources.corwin.com/evidencebasedwriting-fiction.**

Use Eve Bunting as "go to" for theme, because she is a master at symbols and including direct clues. *Gleam and Glow, One Green Apple, Smoky Night, So Far From the Sea, The Wall, Train to Somewhere, The Memory String,* and *Walking to School* are some of my favorites.

Deep in the Bush, Where People Rarely Ever Go: http://www.phillipmartin.info/liberia/homepage2.htm

HOW TO USE THE GRAB AND GO PAGES

- Distribute to students copies of What's the Theme? on page 89 and the folktale "The Mighty" on page 90 as well as several sticky notes.

- In small groups, with a partner, or independently, students read and annotate their thinking on sticky notes.

- Next, have students choose three to five sticky notes to place on the What's the Theme? template.

- Finally, students write a short response. The theme should be stated in a sentence, and students should include a minimum of three facts to support it.

- **On another day**: Have students read a picture book or short story on their own, using the same process you just modeled.

- **Ongoing:** You can reuse this excerpt and make it your own. Use it for character traits, plot, problem, or even dialogue.

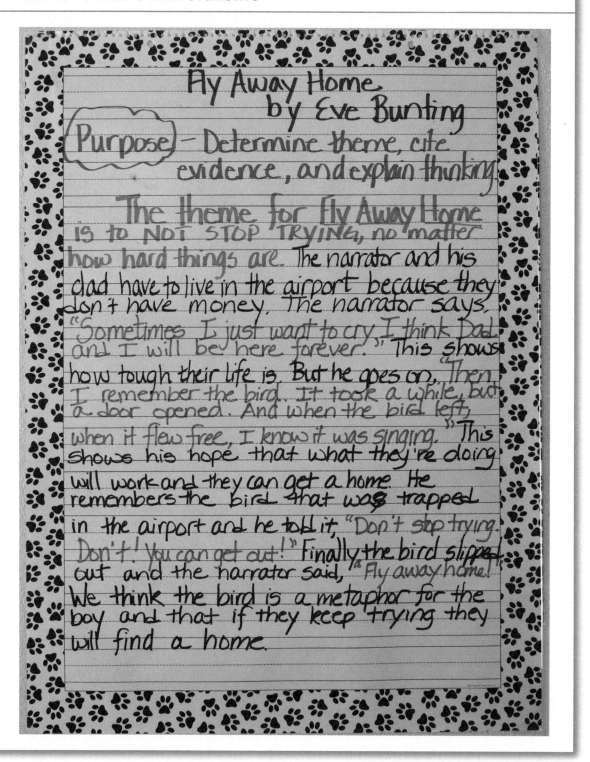

Fly Away Home
by Eve Bunting

Purpose – Determine theme, cite evidence, and explain thinking.

The theme for Fly Away Home is to NOT STOP TRYING, no matter how hard things are. The narrator and his dad have to live in the airport because they don't have money. The narrator says, "Sometimes I just want to cry, I think Dad and I will be here forever." This shows how tough their life is. But he goes on, "Then I remember the bird. It took a while, but a door opened. And when the bird left, when it flew free, I know it was singing." This shows his hope that what they're doing will work and they can get a home. He remembers the bird that was trapped in the airport and he told it, "Don't stop trying. Don't! You can get out!" Finally the bird slipped out and the narrator said, "Fly away home!" We think the bird is a metaphor for the boy and that if they keep trying they will find a home.

What's the Theme?

Name: _____ Date: _____

Title: _____

Directions:

- As you read through the text, use sticky notes to hold your thinking about theme, and include page numbers. Use the prompts to help you.

- After you finish, think about what you think the theme is and revisit the text and your notes. Which details most support the theme and why? Write down the theme and then choose at least three sticky notes to place in the space below. Explain how they support the theme.

- Tie it all together! On a separate piece of paper, write a short summary about the theme.

I think the theme is _____

_____

Support or Evidence	
Sticky With My Jots	How the Details Supports My Thinking About Theme

EXCERPT TO WRITE ABOUT

"The Mighty"

posted by Brishti Bandyopadhyay in Folktales for Kids

Name: _____ Date: _____

▶ Directions:

- **Read through "The Mighty" once to think about the message.**

- **Read a second time and highlight lines that help you name the message/theme.**

- **Annotate your thinking in the margins. How do the lines you highlighted support theme?**

At the edge of a forest, stood a big tree. Its branches spread out majestically and so did its roots. It shielded people from the sun under its shady leaves, and provided shelter to countless birds and other small creatures in its branches. It buzzed with activity all the time.

At the foot of the tree grew a little plant. The plant was willowy and delicate, and tended to keel over at the touch of the slightest breeze.

One day the two neighbors were having a little chat.

"Well, little one," said the tree to the plant, "Why do you not plant your feet deeply in the ground, and raise your head boldly in the air as I do?"

"I see no need to do so," whispered the plant with a smile. "Actually, I think I may be safer this way."

"Safer?" sneered the tree. "Are you suggesting that you're safer than I am? Do you know how deep my roots are buried, how thick and strong my trunk is? Even if two men hold hands they would not be able to surround my trunk. Who could possibly pluck me by the roots or bow my head to the ground?"

And the tree turned away from the plant in a great huff.

But the tree was to regret its words very soon. One evening a great hurricane arose in the region. It hurled the trees off their roots and almost completely destroyed the forest. It uprooted the mean tree and hurled it away with great force.

When the storm had passed, the villagers living nearby surveyed the damage. Mighty trees that had once almost touched the sky were now reduced to stumps or worse. The forest was littered with their carcasses.

But there was one exception. The little plant. The plant had been tossed and turned under the fury of the hurricane, and bent completely. But when the hurricane ended, it sighed and stood upright again.

No trace remained of the mighty neighbor though.

Source: Brishti Bandyopadhyay © Pitara.com

Analyze Development of Theme in Story

BEST THE TEST

- The length of texts used in standardized tests increases as students progress through the grades, so it's good to model and have students practice how one's thinking evolves over the course of a chapter book. During the year, use at least one chapter book to model. After that, students should be reading chapter books all year long!

- Counterintuitively, do a lot of reading for the sheer joy of it! Volume matters, and you can simply ask students to state what they think the theme is, and why.

- When reading chapter books for book clubs or literature circles, students should mark in their book where they find clues about theme. Finally, they write about theme citing evidence.

LESSON PREP

- Read a full-length novel so you know it well. (I use *The Tiger Rising* by Kate DiCamillo in this lesson.) You can either plan to teach the entire novel or just have students work with the excerpts shown on page 94.

- Photocopy Pick a Question (page 93) and the excerpts from *The Tiger Rising* (page 94).

INTRODUCE IT

1. Model thinking about theme with a shared chapter book—in this case *The Tiger Rising*—and show how to hold thinking across a chapter book, either with sticky notes or by recording details and wonderings on chart paper.

2. Or use the novel excerpts on page 94 with five important scenes to focus on if you have less time.

3. Guide students through the text and how it supports theme.

4. Refer to the anchor chart of prompts on page 85 that you created in the previous lesson.

5. As you model, show how your thinking changes over time and *why* it changes.

HOW TO USE THE GRAB AND GO PAGES

- Distribute to students copies of Pick a Question on page 93 and the excerpts from *The Tiger Rising* on page 94.

- There are two options for using these reproducibles:

  - **Option 1:** Have students annotate excerpts from *The Tiger Rising*. These excerpts all include the symbol of the suitcase. Unpack their significance through student discussion, whether in small groups or turn and talk.

  - **Option 2:** Use these excerpts to help you work through a shared reading of the entire novel, *stopping at these points in particular* to discuss theme.

- Students may also respond to these excerpts in their reading journals. If students are working with longer chapter books, respond weekly, using Pick a Question (page 93).

- Have students discuss with partners or in literature circles or book clubs.

- After they finish the book, have students write a summary about theme, analyzing the development and summarizing the key supporting details and ideas.

- **Ongoing:** Repeat these steps with another shared chapter book, and then expect students to transfer these skills to their independent reading and writing, using the prompts to guide them.

- Use the story excerpts on page 94 as the basis for creating your own excerpts page, covering other key moments in DiCamillo's novel. Going forward, do the same thing with other novels. Some favorites for this are *Wonder* by R. J. Palacio, *Because of Mr. Terupt* by Rob Buyea, and *Fish in a Tree* by Lynda Mullaly Hunt.

SAMPLE TO SHARE WITH STUDENTS

Island of the Blue Dolphins *(Theme)*

I think the themes in this book are friendship and survival. I think that because Karana's tribe leaves and she is stuck on the island all alone and she has to learn how to survive. She is waiting for her tribe to come back for her. While she is waiting she is worrying about her enemies--the Aleuts and the wild dogs. After being alone on the island she makes some new friends, too. Not human friends, she makes friends with the animals on the island. They all work together to keep their island safe and fun to be on. She isn't lonely anymore. Even though every animal has to be careful who they are around, Karana can trust them because they have been on the island longer than she has. These friendships help with her survival, so the themes go together. She learns how to survive from the animals and she also tries to protect them. Karana changes from the beginning of the book when she wants to kill the wild dogs in revenge, but then makes friends with the leader and loves him--the two help each other survive. I liked this book because of the themes and how Karana lived in harmony with the animals and was able to survive years of being alone until she was rescued.

Pick a Question

Directions:

- Choose one or more boxes to help you write about the theme in a story you are reading.

- Make sure you give examples from the text to explain your thinking. You can quote what a character says or record sentences.

How do chapter endings help you discover the theme? Which endings in particular?	Which passage from the text do you think is most important? Why do you think this?	Are there symbols or metaphors that help you determine the message? What are they and how do they help?
Does the character learn a lesson? What is the lesson? How might you look at what the main character finally understands for clues about theme? How does this help determine the theme?	What is the big idea or message from the text? (Theme)	Is there repetition? What is it? How does this help to determine theme?
Does the main character ask questions that reveal his inner struggle? How does this help with the big idea?	Does the main character go through important changes? What is/are the change/s? How does this help determine theme?	Does something unexpected happen? Does a character behave differently? How does this help determine theme?

Available for download at **http://resources.corwin.com/evidencebasedwriting-fiction**

EXCERPTS TO WRITE ABOUT

The Tiger Rising

by Kate DiCamillo

▶ We meet Rob under the Kentucky Star Motel sign waiting for the school bus. He is thinking about a tiger he saw in a cage in the woods and then he begins to itch a rash on his leg, which leads him to think of his mother's funeral. His thoughts then turn to a suitcase.

[pp. 3–4]

Rob had a way of not-thinking about things. He imagined himself as a suitcase that was too full, like the one that he had packed when they left Jacksonville after the funeral. He made all his feelings go inside the suitcase, he stuffed them in tight and then sat on the suitcase and locked it shut. That was the way he not-thought about things. Sometimes it was hard to keep the suitcase shut. But now he had something to put on top of it. The tiger.

So as he waited for the bus under the Kentucky Star sign, and as the first drops of rain fell from the sullen sky, Rob imagined the tiger on top of his suitcase, blinking his golden eyes, sitting proud and strong, unaffected by all the not-thoughts inside straining to come out.

▶ As you read this, what are you thinking about Rob? Jot in the margins. Hint: highlight words that repeat! What do you make of the suitcase? Jot ideas, and let's see if the author mentions it again.

▶ After meeting Sistine—a new girl at school—Rob tries to escape the bullies and the pain by thinking of a book that the librarian let him read.

[p. 10]

In the book, the picture from the ceiling of the Sistine Chapel showed God reading out and touching Adam. It was like they were playing a game of tag, like God was making Adam "it." It was a beautiful picture.

Rob looked out the window at the gray rain and the gray sky and the gray highway. He thought about the tiger. He thought about God and Adam. And he thought about Sistine. He did not think about the rash. He did not think about his mother. And he did not think about Norton and Billy Threemonger. He kept the suitcase closed.

▶ Let's look at repetition again. Highlight where you notice that and jot why you think DiCamillo uses it. What do you learn here about Rob? How do you connect his mother's death with his "not-thinking"? If you assume a mother's death is a big event in a child's life, then what details may reveal Rob's response to the event? What do you learn about theme?

[p. 31]

Rob heard the door to the motel room squeak open. He opened his eyes. The world was dark. The only light came from the falling Kentucky Star. Rob turned over in bed

(Continued)

(Continued)

and pulled back the curtain and looked out the window at the sign. It was like having his own personal shooting star, but he didn't ever make a wish on it. He was afraid that if he started wishing, he might not be able to stop. In his suitcase of not-thoughts, there were also not-wishes. He kept the lid closed on them, too.

▶ **What are you thinking about the suitcase now? Why might that give us clues to theme?**

▶ **Because of the rash on his legs, Rob is sent home from school and told not to return until it has cleared up. Rob is friends with Willie May, the housekeeper at the Kentucky Star Motel. As they are working together, she tells him how to cure the rash on his legs. As you read this, think about how it connects to the suitcase.**

> [pp. 37–38]
>
> "Sadness," said Willie May, closing her eyes and nodding her head. "You keeping all that sadness down low, in your legs. You not letting it get up to your heart, where it belongs. You got to let that sadness rise on up."
>
> . . .
>
> "What'd I tell you then?" she said, towering over him. Willie May was tall, the tallest person Rob had ever seen.
>
> "To let the sadness rise," Rob said. He repeated the words as if they were part of a poem. He gave them a certain rhythm, the same way Willie May had when she said them.
>
> "That's right," said Willie May. "You got to let the sadness rise on up."

▶ **What do you notice about repetition in this excerpt? What do you notice about the discussion the characters have? What is your thinking about theme now?**

▶ **The tiger is set free and Rob's father shoots it—to protect the children. This allows Rob to get his hurt and anger toward his father out. It also allows his father to demonstrate his love. While this is not explicitly stated in the text, the reader should infer it from the dialogue and the actions. Rob and Sistine apologize to each other, and she tells him he's her best friend after they decide to bury the tiger and erect a headstone.**

> [p. 117]
>
> The whole way back to the Kentucky Star, Rob held on to Sistine's hand. He marveled at what a small hand it was and how much comfort there was in holding on to it.
>
> And he marveled, too, at how different he felt inside, how much lighter, as if he had set something heavy down and walked away from it, without bothering to look back.

▶ **While there isn't repetition here, think about symbols and what Rob has had inside. What do you notice? How does this give us clues about the theme?**

Note: After this scene, the suitcase is not mentioned again. Guide students to realize that Rob has "opened the suitcase"—or at least left it behind. He's allowed his feelings to rise up and out, too. The heavy weight of sadness is lifted. His wish to have a friend has come true. If you are reading the entire book, discuss the last two pages where Rob's dream provides further expression of the novel's theme. We can't cage our emotions and dreams; we have to embrace them, name them, and also take the risk of setting them free.

Determine Theme in Poetry

Theme: The central message, the lesson, moral, or what the author wants you to come away with in terms of an idea about life or human nature.

PROMPTS FOR DETERMINING THEME IN POETRY

- Are there words that repeat?

- Who's talking? How does point of view help determine the message?

- Does the author keep mentioning a particular object?

- Does the narrator reflect on important memories?

- How does the speaker reflect on a topic?

- Does the title provide clues to the theme?

 Available for download at
http://resources.corwin.com/evidencebasedwriting-fiction

BEST THE TEST

Poetry often shows up on tests since it's short text. Students infer to determine the author's point of view and its effect on theme.

- Have students practice identifying lines that support theme and explaining thinking. Often these lines include figurative language and sensory details.

- Read poetry on a weekly basis so students get used to navigating form and language.

LESSON PREP

- Poetry is accessible, and students can work through a piece in a single sitting. Song lyrics are engaging, high interest, and only a click away online. Choose a song such as Christina Aguilera's "Beautiful," which contains a message that students can relate to. Ahead of the lesson make photocopies of the lyrics, or project them on a whiteboard. Have the song downloaded so students can listen to it.

INTRODUCE IT

1. Distribute prompts to students and/or display them on the wall as an anchor chart.

2. Also create your own anchor chart with the prompts. Project lyrics and highlight/think aloud on a whiteboard, or distribute copies to students to work along with you. Read through once with the purpose of looking for the message.

3. Discuss the author's point of view (in the case of "Beautiful," that sometimes she hurts, but won't let words bring her down, that she'll still believe that she's beautiful). Are there words that repeat? ("Words can't bring me down.") Continue by asking questions that prompt readers to notice theme and how the answers help determine the message. Highlight lines and words as you discuss—annotate thinking. What do you infer as you read/listen to this? Why is "Beautiful" the title?

4. **Write about reading:** Co-construct a short response stating the theme and *why* you think this. Be explicit and list what lines helped determine this both literally and inferentially. Include or cite *more than one example*. State the theme in a sentence.

5. Tell students they will be doing this same process you are now modeling, answering the question: What was the theme and what details or lines in the text helped you determine that?

For students who need more structure and support, download Think About Theme in Poetry from **http://resources.corwin.com/evidence basedwriting-fiction.**

Any poetry books by Douglas Florian are glorious for teaching theme.

Jane Yolen's poetry books are also wonderful.

A Child's Anthology of Poetry edited by Elizabeth Hauge Sword

Reader's Theater Classic Poetry by Susan Brown

You can search online for any song.

- "Beautiful" by Christina Aguilera (including the lyrics): https://youtu.be/ VYmFpYdwqLs

- Lyrics to "A Place in the World" by Taylor Swift: http://www.azlyrics. com/lyrics/taylorswift/ aplaceinthisworld.html

HOW TO USE THE GRAB AND GO PAGES

- Distribute to students copies of Find the Evidence on page 99 and "Mr. Nobody" on page 100.

- Students highlight and annotate, using the same process you just modeled. Reinforce using the anchor chart to guide the process.

- **On another day:** Repeat the lesson using popular song lyrics. If you have the technology available—computers, iPads, and headphones—have links available for students to listen to various songs. Have lyrics printed out. This allows for student choice and/or differentiation. If technology is not available, have lyrics printed ahead of time.

- **Ongoing:** You can reuse the Find the Evidence template whenever you work with theme in poetry (or in other genres).

SAMPLE TO SHARE WITH STUDENTS

"Beautiful"
by Christina Aguilera

Purpose Theme in Poetry

The lyrics to "Beautiful" are poetry. The speaker's point of view is that sometimes she's insecure or ashamed, but she won't let others' words "bring her down" or ruin her self concept, and she'll still believe she's "beautiful." That fits with the theme. Have confidence and believe in yourself; you're beautiful inside and out and don't let words convince you otherwise. The repetition of:
"I am beautiful" (you're beautiful, we're...)
"In every single way"
Shows how to think positively along with:
"We're the song inside the tune"
"And everywhere we go
The sun will always shine"
shows hope. The repetition of:
"yes, words can't bring me (you, us) down"
Shows how to rise above others' negative comments. The title reinforces the theme that we are all beautiful and unique.

Find the Evidence

Name: _____   Date: _____

Title: _____

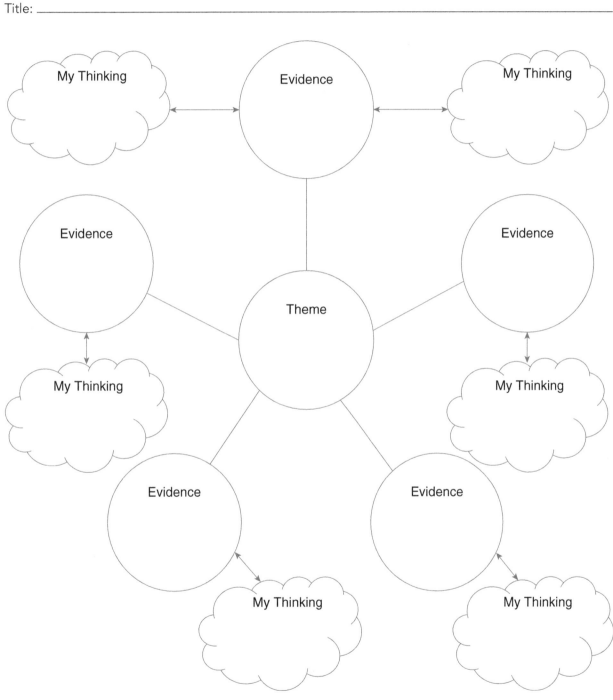

My Thinking

Evidence

My Thinking

Evidence

Theme

Evidence

My Thinking

My Thinking

Evidence

Evidence

My Thinking

My Thinking

EXCERPT TO WRITE ABOUT

"Mr. Nobody"

by Anonymous

Name: _____ Date: _____

▶ Directions:

- Read "Mr. Nobody" and think about who is narrating the poem and the message.

- Were there details that helped? Highlight these and write a few notes about what you are thinking.

- Were there any words you didn't know? Highlight these and see if you can figure out their meaning by the context.

> I know a funny little man who's as quiet as a mouse,
>
> Who does the mischief that is done in everybody's house!
>
> There's no one ever sees his face, and yet we all agree
>
> That every plate we break was cracked by Mr. Nobody.
>
> 'Tis he who always tears our books, who leaves the door ajar,
>
> He pulls the buttons from our shirts and scatters pins afar.
>
> That squeaking door will always squeak—forever! 'Cause you see
>
> We leave its oiling to be done by Mr. Nobody.
>
> The fingerprints upon the door by none of us are made.
>
> We never leave the blinds unclosed to let the curtains fade.
>
> The milk we never spill; the boots that laying 'round you see
>
> Are not our boots! They belong to Mr. Nobody.

Questions:

What is the theme of "Mr. Nobody"? What in the text supports your thinking?

_____

_____

_____

_____

_____

_____

_____

(Continued)

(Continued)

Does the title provide clues to the theme?

_____

_____

_____

_____

_____

_____

_____

Are there words that repeat?

_____

_____

_____

_____

_____

_____

_____

Who's talking? How does point of view help determine the message?

_____

_____

_____

_____

_____

_____

_____

Compare and Contrast
Theme in Poetry

BEST THE TEST

Compare and contrast is prevalent in testing, including comparing poetry to other genres. Poetry requires inferences and thinking, which transfers to tests. Here's a tip:

- Students should be exposed to poetry for the sheer joy of reading and writing it, *not* just for test prep!

LESSON PREP

- A great way to "amp up" instruction on poetry is to have students work through more complex poems, asking and answering questions independently when determining theme as well as comprehending and responding to poetry.

- Photocopy and distribute "Dreams" and "Mother to Son" by Langston Hughes *or*

- Photocopy two poems on the same topic. For example, any books by Douglas Florian include poetry on the same topic (winter, fall, spring, mammals, etc.).

INTRODUCE IT

1. Model thinking about theme in poetry with two different pieces, and compare and contrast them (in this case "Dreams" and "Mother to Son," both by Langston Hughes).

2. Highlight and annotate as you guide students through the first poem, and then the second poem, to determine theme.

3. Refer to the prompts on page 96 and make sure students have them.

4. As you model, show how your thinking changes over time and *why* it changes.

5. Discuss how the themes of the two poems are similar and how they differ.

6. Fill out the Elements of Poetry template.

7. **Write about reading:** Co-construct a short response comparing and contrasting *theme* in the poems. Use the template to scaffold writing. State the themes in sentence form and cite evidence from the text to support thinking.

8. Tell students they will be doing this same process you are now modeling, answering the questions: What are the themes? How are they similar? How are they different? What details in the text helped you determine that?

For students who may need more structure and support, download the Compare/Contrast Poetry organizer from **http://resources.corwin.com/ evidencebasedwriting-fiction.**

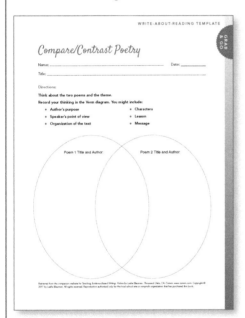

A beautiful nonfiction picture book is *Coming Home, From the Life of Langston Hughes* by Floyd Cooper, which provides background for the poems included in this lesson.

BookSpeak! Poems About Books by Laura Purdie Salas

Novels in verse:

● *Love That Dog* and *Hate That Cat* by Sharon Creech

● *Locomotion* and *Brown Girl Dreaming* by Jacqueline Woodson

● *The Crossover* by Kwame Alexander

Authors performing reader's theater of their books: http://www.teachingbooks.net/ author_collection.cgi?id=1&a=1

HOW TO USE THE GRAB AND GO PAGES

- Tell students they will be reading two poems by the same author. They will use what they already know about determining theme as they read each.

- Distribute to students copies of Elements of Poetry on page 105 and the first poem, "Dreams" on page 106.

- Using the prompts on page 96, have students highlight and annotate their thinking and discuss as a class.

- Do the same with the second poem, "Mother to Son." This may require more co-constructing/teacher guidance due to language.

- Have students fill out the Elements of Poetry template *together*, and step in if they need your assistance.

- **Ongoing:** Use the Elements of Poetry template as the basis for student response to poetry—not just writing about theme.

- Give students practice with poetry on a regular basis. Students can respond in their reading journals or write in response to the Elements of Poetry template. This form combines different aspects/elements of poetry into one written response.

Elements of Poetry

Directions:

Fill out the tree with your thinking and evidence from the text that shows how you know. Finally, write a summary at the base that includes the message.

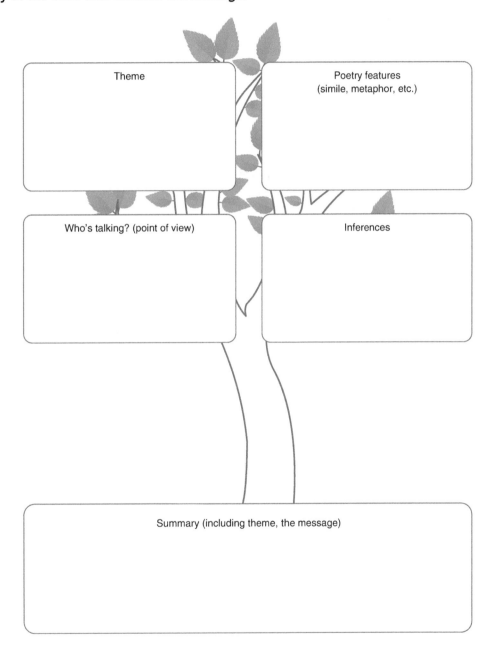

Theme

Poetry features
(simile, metaphor, etc.)

Who's talking? (point of view)

Inferences

Summary (including theme, the message)

EXCERPTS TO WRITE ABOUT

"Dreams"

by Langston Hughes

Hold fast to dreams

For if dreams die

Life is a broken-winged bird

That cannot fly.

Hold fast to dreams

For when dreams go

Life is a barren field

Frozen with snow.

"Mother to Son"

by Langston Hughes

Well, son, I'll tell you,

Life for me ain't been no crystal stair.

It's had tacks in it,

And splinters,

And boards torn up,

And places with no carpet on the floor—

Bare.

But all the time

I'se been a-climbin' on

And reachin' landin's,

And turnin' corners,

And sometimes goin' in the dark

Where there ain't been no light.

So, boy, don't you turn back.

Don't you set down on the steps

'Cause you finds it kinder hard.

Don't you fall now—

For I'se still goin', honey,

I'se still climbin',

And life for me ain't been no crystal stair.

SECTION 4

Point of View

Perhaps one of the most common test questions is "What was the author's purpose in writing this piece?" The answer choices are usually *to persuade, to inform,* or *to entertain.* Once in a while *to express* or *to explain and describe* is included on the exams.

The tricky thing is, authors rarely write and publish with a single, clear-cut purpose in mind. When I think of fiction, nonfiction, and memoir authors today—Jon Krakauer, Anne Lamott, and Elizabeth Gilbert are three favorites out of two hundred!—I consider them writers whose narrative structure and prose are so sterling that surely their purpose was to inform *and* to entertain. And to complicate the concept of purpose even more, persuasion often plays into all genres. That is, it is hard to write without a semblance of persuasion, your own perspective, seeping into the prose. That's where point of view (POV) enters, and in the classroom we can use POV as an entryway to students' thinking about an author's purpose. In literature, we focus largely on characters' points of view. Discerning the author's point of view often comes after that and is part of culminating discussions about a work.

As you will see in the lessons in this section, I often start by awakening *students'* point of view. This gives them something to weigh against what the author seems to be saying. Discovering how *they* are feeling or whether they are believing/disbelieving the point of view of a character in a text helps them read critically and question. Once they can do this, students can compare and contrast their point of view with others' and also compare and contrast across books or across characters.

Students need to support their thinking by using examples from the text or from illustrations, which can be terrific for building inferential thinking. (Note: The lessons here overlap with the lessons in Section 5, Visuals, that begins on page 133.)

Students need to be familiar with terms related to point of view and to know if something is written in first person (I, me), third person (he, she, they), or second person (you). As you share these lessons, explicitly make the point that *how* the story is told affects how the events are portrayed.

Other terms students should be working on consistently are *narrator* (the one telling the story in a novel or work of short fiction) and *speaker* (what one generally calls the voice of the poem, but which one should not assume is the author). Finally, knowing the difference between *perspective* and *point of view* is helpful. *Perspective* is the scene as viewed through the eyes or seen through the mind of a specific character chosen by the author. The story can be told from one or a variety of points of view and can be different from each character's perspective.

Watch Leslie Teach!

Video 4: **Watch Leslie guide students to notice and write about point of view in a text.**

Go to **http://resources.corwin.com/evidencebasedwriting-fiction** to see the lessons and guided practice in action.

Whose Point of View Is It?

Point of View: The place, vantage point, or consciousness through which we hear or see someone describe a situation, tell a story, or make an argument. Different POVs are distinguished by how much the narrator or reporter knows: first person (I, me); third person (he, she, they); an *omniscient* POV knows what everyone thinks and feels; a *limited* POV knows only so much about a character or knows only what one character (out of many) thinks; and an *unreliable* narrator is not trustworthy. In some cases multiple POVs can be used or represented within one text.

PROMPTS FOR LOOKING AT POINT OF VIEW

- Who is telling the story and *why*?

- How does this affect the narration?

- How does the narrator's or speaker's point of view affect the description of events and other characters?

- Why might the author tell the story from this point of view?

- What techniques or devices does the author use to develop the point of view of the speaker or narrator?

 Available for download at
http://resources.corwin.com/evidencebasedwriting-fiction

BEST THE TEST

Students are required to determine the author's purpose across a variety of text types on tests, and because point of view is often intertwined with a fiction author's purpose, it's a literary element students need to know. Here are specific tasks to practice with students that show up on tests:

- Retell or rewrite the story from different characters' points of view.

- Compare and contrast different points of view.

LESSON PREP

- Make photocopies of Point of View (page 112) and the *I Am the Dog I Am the Cat* excerpts (page 114).

- Choose a book with a distinguishable point of view. For this lesson, I use Mark Teague's *Dear Mrs. LaRue: Letters From Obedience School.* Familiarize yourself with the format. For example, in this book, Ike, the dog, is trying to persuade his owner how awful obedience school is through his letters and the black-and-white illustrations. However, the colored illustrations offer a different perspective! In addition, newspaper articles are added to show an impartial perspective.

INTRODUCE IT

1. Distribute prompts to students and/or display them on the wall as an anchor chart.

2. Also create your own anchor chart with the prompts.

3. Before reading aloud the story, let students know that the *purpose* of the lesson is to determine the main character's point of view and *why* they think that, and to notice and name what the author does to show the character's point of view. (In this book, Mark Teague is both author and illustrator, so students should use both text and illustrations.)

4. Read aloud *Dear Mrs. LaRue* (or whichever book you've chosen), determining right away if the book is written in first person or third person. In the case of *Dear Mrs. LaRue*, the first page is a newspaper article, followed by letters from Ike (the dog). The article is in third person; the letters are in first person.

5. Think aloud on the first page about Ike's point of view and what in the text makes you think that (e.g., Ike doesn't like obedience school).

6. Allow students to recognize the differences between the black-and-white illustrations and the colored ones, and discuss why Mark Teague did that. (The black-and-white illustrations show what Ike wants Mrs. LaRue to think; the colored pictures depict reality.)

7. After reading a few pages, refer to prompts on the anchor chart and jot down student thinking and answers. The main question to discuss is "How does the narrator's or speaker's point of view affect the description of events in the text?" Tell students that as you finish the book, they should see if they agree with these initial thoughts, or if they want to change them (point to emphasize: Teague using exaggeration and humor to enhance the point of view).

8. Finish reading the book and return to the chart and discuss.

9. **Write about reading:** Choose one of the prompts from the anchor chart and write in greater depth, referring to evidence in the text. Or, if using *Dear Mrs. LaRue*, have students write about the differences between the first person and third person sections and how that affected their understanding. Why did the author decide to format the book this way?

10. This lesson can be replicated using the follow-up books by Mark Teague (*Detective LaRue: Letters From the Investigation, LaRue for Mayor: Letters From the Campaign Trail, LaRue Across America: Postcards From the Vacation*).

For students who may need more support, download the POV Summarizer from **http://resources.corwin .com/evidencebasedwriting-fiction**.

WRITE-ABOUT-READING TEMPLATE

POV Summarizer

Name: _____ Date: _____

Title: _____

Thinking About Point of View (POV)

This story is told in _____ (first person, second person, third person).

_____ is telling the story.

The point of view is _____

I know this because in the text it states _____

Another reason is _____

A final reason is _____

The point of view affected the events because _____

Encounter by Jane Yolen

Memoirs of a Goldfish by Devin Scillian

How to Babysit a Grandma and *How to Babysit a Grandpa* by Jean Reagan

BookSpeak! Poems About Books by Laura Purdie Salas

Heroes by Ken Mochizuki

For diverging POV on WWII:

- *Baseball Saved Us* by Ken Mochizuki

- *Passage to Freedom* by Ken Mochizuki

- *So Far From the Sea* by Eve Bunting

- *The Bracelet* by Yoshiko Uchida

Monsterbox: https://youtu.be/DoLAoOkG5gY

Hapless Hamster: https://youtu.be/w1aDcjqYBNI

Home Sweet Home: https://youtu.be/aKRZn0uS6eA

Rock, Paper, Scissors: https://youtu.be/UYxpX3N20qU

HOW TO USE THE GRAB AND GO PAGES

- Distribute to students copies of Point of View on page 112 and the *I Am the Dog I Am the Cat* excerpts on page 114. Another option is to read aloud the picture book as you work through the excerpts.

- Have students work alone or with partners to determine point of view.

- To have students practice *writing* from a variety of points of view, use the chart on page 112. Place a photo or text in the center and have students write about the photo in first person (one character), another character as first person, and then third person. In addition, students write what the reader's *perspective* is.

- Alternatively, select an illustration from one of the LaRue books (or any other picture book) to use. (For older students, use the Point of View: Advanced template on page 113.)

- **Ongoing:** Determining the author's purpose and point of view should become a natural and authentic part of reading all books. Students should internalize the prompts. However, as you introduce new genres or more sophisticated material, refer back to these prompts—especially *how the author develops point of view*. Look at first person child narrator and contrast it with an adult narrator. Deepen point of view work by looking at it through the lens of word choice as well as point of view in inner monologues and in dialogue.

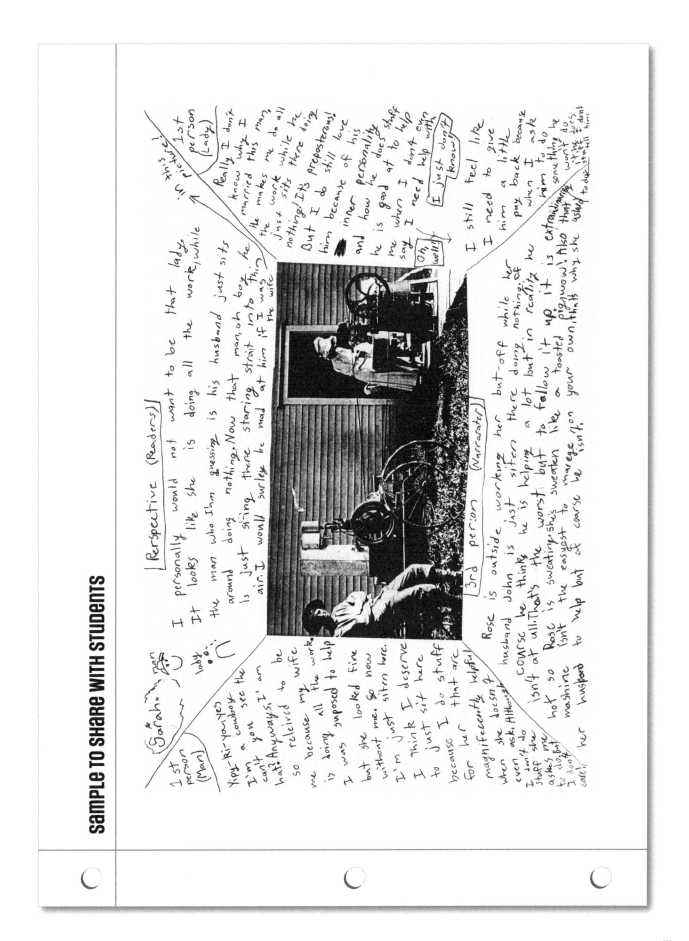

Perspective (Readers)

1st person (Man)

Yipy-Ki-yay yes I'm a cowboy can't you see the hat. Anyways, I am so releived to be doing all the work because my wife is supposed to help me. I was looked fine but she looked fine now without me. So now I'm just sitten here. I think I deserve to just sit here because I do stuff that are for her that are magnificently helpful when she doesn't even ask. Although I don't stuff me asks me to do but I don't care! her husband

I personally would not want to be that lady. It looks like she is doing all the work, while the man who I'm guessing is his husband just sits around doing nothing. Now that man, oh boy, he is just sitting there staring strait into thin air. I would surley be mad at him if I the wife

1st person (Lady)

Really I don't know why I married this man? He makes me do all the work while he just sits there doing nothing! It's preposterous! But I do still love him because of his inner personality and how he does stuff he is good at to help me when I need don't even help him with. I just don't know!

Oh well!

I still feel like I need to give him a little pay back because when I ask him to do something he won't do it. He does it like a toasted pig wow! Also that's extraordinary why she asked to our stuff I don't tell him

3rd person (Narrator)

Rose is outside working her but-off while her husband John is just sitten there doing nothing. Of course he thinks he is helping a lot but in reality he isn't at all. That's the worst but to follow it up Rose is sweating, she's sweaten like a hot so Rose isn't the easyest to marege mashine isn't the easyest to help but of coarse he isn't. on your own that's why she husband

iii

Point of View

Name: _____

Title: _____

Date: _____

Perspective

First person (character)

First person (different character)

Insert picture here

Third person

Available for download at http://resources.corwin.com/evidencebasedwriting-fiction

Point of View: Advanced

Name: _____ Date: _____

Title: _____

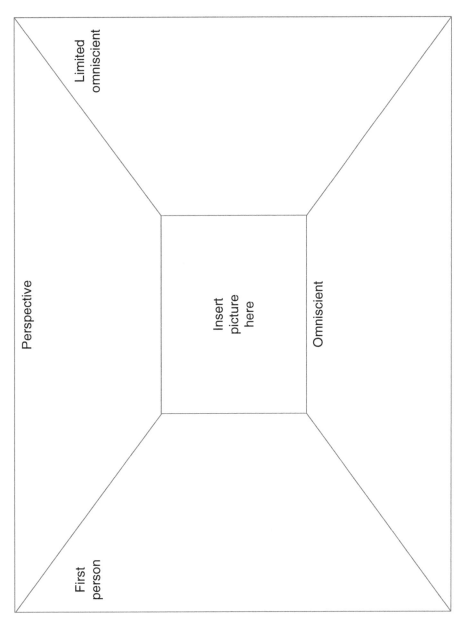

Perspective

Limited omniscient

First person

Insert picture here

Omniscient

Available for download at **http://resources.corwin.com/evidencebasedwriting-fiction**

EXCERPTS TO WRITE ABOUT

I Am the Dog I Am the Cat

by Donald Hall

▶ As you meet the dog and the cat, think about if this is written in first, second, or third person. How do you know? Why do you think the author decided to write the book this way? What techniques does the author use to develop the point of view of each character? Highlight words and phrases that help you determine this.

Dog: I am the dog.

I like bones.

I like to *bury* bones.

As for eating, I can take it or leave it—

But I like it when *they* feed me.

Cat: I am the cat.

I don't *care* whether they feed me or not

as long as I get fed.

Sometimes I tease them to feed me,

then turn up my nose at what I get.

▶ What have you learned about the two characters' personalities from this first page? How would you describe the point of view of each? Write your thinking in the margins.

Dog: I sleep all day in order to stay rested,

in order to be alert

when it is my duty to bark.

Cat: I sleep all day

in order to stay awake all night

on mouse patrol.

Dog: After I sleep all day,

I sleep all night, for

I am the dog.

(Continued)

(Continued)

Cat: Cats work hard.

When people and dogs are asleep,

I never stop hunting mice,

I hunt pieces of paper, paper clips, or

rubber bands.

▶   **Has your opinion of each character changed? How does each character view sleep and work? Write your thinking in the margins.**

▶   **In this final excerpt, think about how each describes the other and himself or herself. How does this fit with each character's perspective? As you read, are there any words that you don't know? Make sure to mark them, as they add to the character description.**

Cat: Dogs are nervous and well-meaning.

It is well-known that cats

are at the same time

independent,

selfish,

fearless,

beautiful,

cuddly,

scratchy,

and intelligent.

Dog: Cats don't *care.*

Only a dog

is at the same time

dignified,

guilty,

sprightly,

obedient,

friendly,

vigilant,

and soulful.

▶   **After reading these three excerpts do you agree with the cat's point of view? Why? Do you agree with the dog's? Why? If their owner was to write a description for each of these sections, what do you think they would say? Choose one of these questions and write a response.**

Note: Donald Hall uses the form of alternating character monologues to structure his poem/play. It's published in the form of a picture book, with gorgeous illustrations by Barry Moser that accentuate the contrasts between the feline and the canine. Hall zeroes in on the essential traits of dogs ("I like bones") and cats ("Cat's don't *care*"), and this makes the work a terrific model for talking about character traits. His use of adjectives, including unusual ones like *scratchy* and *sprightly*, remind us about the importance of word choice in making a character's personalities come to life.

How Point of View Colors the Way a Story Is Told

BEST THE TEST

In testing situations students determine point of view in short pieces of text or in excerpts, thus periodic practice is helpful. Here are some specific practice ideas:

- Although tests rely heavily on short pieces, in real-life reading students need to learn how point of view *evolves and changes* over the course of a novel. Thus, don't shy away from helping students see the whole span of a character's perspective, because it will serve them well on tests. Any novel worth its salt is going to treat readers to characters who go through a remarkable change.

- When reading chapter books independently, students should also keep an eye out for *author's* purpose and point of view, especially noticing the techniques that authors use (humor, dialogue, inner dialogue or thoughts, irony, key questions, etc.).

LESSON PREP

- Photocopy Who Is Telling the Story? (page 119) and "My First Step to the White House" (page 120).

- Read a full-length novel so you know it well and discuss at various junctures the point of view and perspective of the characters. Discuss how point of view influences how the events in the story are told.

- Display a chart you add to of techniques authors use to help the reader determine point of view (humor, dialogue, inner dialogue or thoughts, irony, key questions, etc.).

- Share the prompts with students.

INTRODUCE IT

1. Model thinking about author's purpose and point of view with a shared chapter book or read-aloud book.

2. Or use "My First Step to the White House" (page 120) to discern point of view, and cite from the text where the author shows it. Do this either as a guided lesson or in small groups or independently.

More information on *The One and Only Ivan*:

- http://theoneandonlyivan.com
- http://www.npr.org/ 2013/06/13/191053327/ headline-here

The Watsons Go to Birmingham by Christopher Paul Curtis

The One and Only Ivan by Katherine Applegate

Crenshaw by Katherine Applegate

Walk Two Moons by Sharon Creech

Sweet Cocoon: https://youtu.be/D0a0aNqTehM

Presto!: Do an online search for Pixar's "Presto!"

Ivan the Beloved Gorilla: https://youtu.be/fCuFU2RdUGc

HOW TO USE THE GRAB AND GO PAGES

- Distribute to students copies of Who Is Telling the Story? on page 119 and "My First Step to the White House" on page 120.

- Have students work individually or with a partner to read the story and jot down their thinking in the margins.

- Encourage students to refer back to the prompts that help determine point of view.

- Next, have students complete the Who is Telling the Story? template.

- **On another day:** Have students either write about the narrator and his point of view OR rewrite the story from the father's point of view.

- **Ongoing:** Repeat this task periodically, using short stories or chapters from book club or literature circle books.

- When conferring with students or working in small groups, frequently ask about point of view and how the author shows that in the text.

SAMPLE TO SHARE WITH STUDENTS

From *My First Step to the White House* by Chris Van Allsburg

As you begin, think about who is telling the story and how that affects the point of view you will be getting on the events. Highlight words that support the point of view and jot notes.

first person

When I was about nine years old, my father bought me a go-kart. It was fire-engine red and had a chain-saw motor on the back that was a screaming terror

My family lived in a neighborhood where there were winding dirt roads, and it wasn't long before I was blasting through turns sideways, kicking up a rooster tail of gravel. *— loves it!*

The roads weren't the only thing that was dirt. So were the driveways. But one morning an asphalt truck pulled up to our house, and by the afternoon our dusty, rutted drive had been transformed into a ribbon of smooth black perfection, the envy of the neighborhood. *— That will be fun*

A few days later my mom and dad had to go out for the afternoon. Before they left, my dad reminded me of an agreement that we'd made: I would never, ever, use the kart if he wasn't around. If I did, no more go-kart. *promised Dad*

After my parents left, my friend Steve came over. One thing led to another, and pretty soon we were rolling the kart out of the drive. I figured one little ride wouldn't hurt. Besides, my dad would never know. *'uH oH!'*

Doesn't think he'll get caught

How do you think the narrator's point of view will affect what happens? What leads you to think that? *He's going to break his promise* *No one will know.*

I checked the gas tank on the kart. Empty. We kept the extra gas in a giant ten-gallon army surplus gas can. Steve and I dragged the full can across the driveway and lifted it up. Unfortunately, it was too heavy for us. We ended up pouring one gallon into the cart and about nine gallons onto the driveway. *big problem*

Do you now what happens to fresh asphalt when gasoline gets on it? Neither did I. It turns into a gooey black muck and sort of melts away. Steve and I stared at the crater in my driveways like it was a chemistry experiment gone very wrong.

I knew I was in big trouble. Not only had I broken my promise about not using the go-kart, I'd also messed up our brand new driveway. I felt so bad; I just rolled the kart back into the garage. *important →*

BIG! ✱ He knows he messed up.

I waited for my parents to come home, feeling worse every minute. Finally, they pulled into the driveway and parked right over the hole. They hadn't noticed it. Was I lucky! *← Will he tell?*

I knew when my dad discovered the hole, he'd ask me about it. I'd blame it on the car. Everybody knows cars leak, right? *Going to lie?*

Who Is Telling the Story?

Name: _____ Date: _____

Title: _____

Who is telling the story?
How I know:

This is the point of view:

How I know this (citing evidence)	
Page number and evidence to show the narrator's POV about events	Explanation

Choose one of the questions below and write a response:

- How does the narrator view the events?
- Choose a different character from the story. How would things be different if the same event was told from this character's perspective?
- Rewrite the story from a different character's POV.

Available for download at **http://resources.corwin.com/evidencebasedwriting-fiction**

EXCERPTS TO WRITE ABOUT

"My First Step to the White House"

by Chris Van Allsburg

▶ **As you begin, think about who is telling the story and how that affects the point of view you will be getting on the events. Highlight words that support the point of view and jot notes.**

When I was about nine years old, my father bought me a go-kart. It was fire-engine red and had a chain-saw motor on the back that was a screaming terror.

My family lived in a neighborhood where there were winding dirt roads, and it wasn't long before I was blasting through turns sideways, kicking up a rooster tail of gravel.

The roads weren't the only thing that was dirt. So were the driveways. But one morning an asphalt truck pulled up to our house, and by the afternoon our dusty, rutted drive had been transformed into a ribbon of smooth black perfection, the envy of the neighborhood.

A few days later my mom and dad had to go out for the afternoon. Before they left, my dad reminded me of an agreement that we'd made: I would never, ever, use the kart if he wasn't around. If I did, no more go-kart.

After my parents left, my friend Steve came over. One thing led to another, and pretty soon we were rolling the kart out of the drive. I figured one little ride wouldn't hurt. Besides, my dad would never know.

▶ **How do you think the narrator's point of view will affect what happens? What leads you to think that?**

I checked the gas tank on the kart. Empty. We kept the extra gas in a giant ten-gallon army surplus gas can. Steve and I dragged the full can across the driveway and lifted it up. Unfortunately, it was too heavy for us. We ended up pouring one gallon into the cart and about nine gallons onto the driveway.

Do you know what happens to fresh asphalt when gasoline gets on it? Neither did I. It turns into a gooey black muck and sort of melts away. Steve and I stared at the crater in my driveway like it was a chemistry experiment gone very wrong.

I knew I was in big trouble. Not only had I broken my promise about not using the go-kart, I'd also messed up our brand-new driveway. I felt so bad; I just rolled the kart back into the garage.

I waited for my parents to come home, feeling worse every minute. Finally, they pulled into the driveway and parked right over the hole. They hadn't noticed it. Was I lucky!

I knew when my dad discovered the hole, he'd ask me about it. I'd blame it on the car. Everybody knows cars leak, right?

▶ **How are the narrator's thinking and feelings emerging and changing? What are you thinking of the main character?**

My mom fixed dinner, but I didn't have much of an appetite. In fact, I was starting to feel pretty bad. The idea of waiting until someone discovered the hole and then lying

(Continued)

about it was too much for me. I couldn't take it. Before we had dessert, I dragged my dad out to the driveway and confessed. I think I may have started crying a little bit, too. My dad moved the car and looked at the hole. "Well," he said, "that's not too bad. Let's go back in and have some ice cream."

My dad did end up taking the kart away, but only for a few weeks. When I went to my room that night I felt pretty lucky. Lying I bed, I realized I'd heard about this sort of thing happening before. I'm sure you have heard the story, too. It's called "Parson Weems' Fable," and it tells how young George Washington cut down a cherry tree. When his father discovered the fallen tree, George said, "I cannot tell a lie, Father, I did it with my little hatchet."

George escaped the worse punishment he might have gotten, because he'd told the truth. "Golly," I thought, "I just did that myself!" I fell asleep wondering if one day I'd be president, too.

▶ **How does the end of this tie to the title? How does the narrator's point of view relate to that?**

Note: Chris Van Allsburg focuses his story on a situation that just about anyone, no matter what age, can relate to. Who hasn't in childhood done something against the rules and then been tempted to cover it up? With the line "I figured one little ride wouldn't hurt. Besides, my dad would never know" the author captures the very reasoning we might use when engaging in a risky act of some kind. Notice, too, the way the author captures the physical sensations of being in trouble, guilt, and being braced for when one's crime is discovered: "feeling worse every minute"; "I didn't have much of an appetite." Not only do these details help us connect to this young person, but they also reveal things about his character. Clearly, he is not prone to lying and feels so guilty that he owns up to what he did—before it is discovered.

In this story, the point of view is that of a young boy trying to navigate the sometimes fuzzy boundaries between obeying parents and having independent adventures. Words like *screaming terror, blasting, never ever,* and *big trouble* remind us that we are hearing the story from "inside the head" of youth. The boy does something he promised not to do, covers up his wrongdoing at first, and then tells the truth. As students discuss this story, help them understand the concept of point of view by asking: What might have been different if the father told this story? How might the friend have told it if it had been written from the father's point of view?

Compare and Contrast Narration in Different Texts

Multiple Viewpoints: The story is told by only one character at a time, but the viewpoint character switches between two or more characters throughout the course of the text. It adds to the story to have it told from different points of view because the reader gains insight into a variety of characters and sees their perspective about the events, problems, and other characters.

PROMPTS FOR COMPARING AND CONTRASTING NARRATION IN DIFFERENT TEXTS

- Is the text written in first person or third person?

- How does this affect the narration and the point of view?

- Who is telling the story in each text and *why*?

- What point of view does the narrator take in each text?

- How are these stories similar? How are they different?

- Why does the author tell the story from these different characters' perspectives?

- What techniques does the author use to develop and distinguish between the different characters' or narrators' points of view?

Available for download at
http://resources.corwin.com/evidencebasedwriting-fiction

BEST THE TEST

Comparing and contrasting is a major focus of testing. Students are asked to compare within texts and across texts.

- In addition, students are asked to read a text and then write a response from a different character's point of view. Therefore, providing students with ample practice identifying and comparing different characters is beneficial.

- Literature written from the viewpoint of a variety of characters has become popular and is engaging for students. It also provides the opportunity to interact and think critically about the text.

LESSON PREP

- Choose a book with multiple characters telling the story. (For this lesson, I use Drew Daywalt's *The Day the Crayons Quit*.)

- Create an anchor chart with the characters' names in the left column and room on the right to record their point of view OR create a sheet for students to fill out as you read.

INTRODUCE IT

1. Distribute prompts to students and/or display them on the wall as an anchor chart.

2. Also create your own anchor chart with the prompts.

3. Begin by stating the purpose—to define different characters' points of view and why they think this.

4. Because *The Day the Crayons Quit* is hilarious, read through once for the sheer enjoyment of the text and to let students experience the entire story.

5. Before reading a second time, ask how the book is written (first person) and why the author chose that.

6. Read through again, stopping at the different characters and discussing (e.g., red needs a rest because he's used all the time, purple needs to stay within the lines, beige feels that he's second to brown). Either record on the anchor chart or co-construct with students.

7. **Write about reading:** Have students write in response to these questions: Why does the author tell the story from these different characters' perspectives? What techniques does the author use to develop and distinguish between the different characters' or narrators' points of view? (humor!)

Access the Character Chart for *The Day the Crayons Quit* by Drew Daywalt from **http://resources.corwin.com/evidencebasedwriting-fiction.**

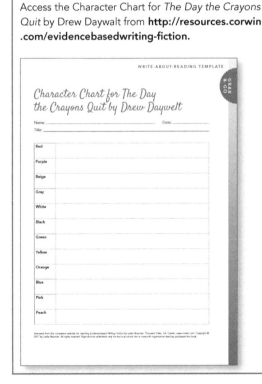

The Day the Crayons Quit and The Day the Crayons Came Home by Drew Daywalt

What Mess? by Tom Lichtenheld (another great book to show two sides to the story, the boy's and his parents')

Fractured fairy tales and the originals (see *The Common Core Companion: Booster Lessons, Grades 3–5* [Blauman, 2015] for more information on this)

Nettie's Trip South by Ann Turner

Pink and Say by Patricia Polacco

Mirror, Mirror by Marilyn Singer

Day and Night: https://youtu.be/QH90a_nJUAE

Sleeping Beauty (or any of the Disney cartoons) and *Maleficent*

HOW TO USE THE GRAB AND GO PAGES

- Distribute to each student copies of Compare POV on page 125 and the Medusa stories on pages 126–127.

- Students can work individually or in pairs to fill in the chart and write about author's purpose and comparing points of view across texts.

- **Ongoing:** Have students do more practice with *The Day the Crayons Came Home*, the follow-up book to *The Day the Crayons Quit*.

- Encourage students to discover other books that are narrated by more than one character and share them with the class.

- Move from comparing characters *within* a text to characters *across* texts. Fairy tales and myths are great for this.

- You can use this comparison chart as you continue to study additional texts and differing points of view. In addition, you can make it your own and use it to compare different aspects of literature.

MORE TEMPLATES TO SHARE WITH STUDENTS

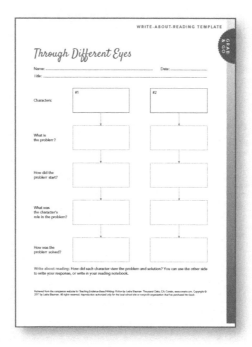

 Available for download at **http://resources.corwin.com/evidencebasedwriting-fiction**

Compare POV

Name: _____ Date: _____

Title:_____

| Title 1 | ←→ | Title 2 |

Narrator

| | ←→ | |

Perspective/POV

↓   ↓

| | | |

Characters

| | |

Problem and Cause

| | |

Explain how the narrator's POV affects the description and how events are explained.

| Events | | Events |

EXCERPTS TO WRITE ABOUT

"Medusa, Pegasus, and the Chimera"
retold by Steven Zorn

▶ **Read this excerpt from a classic myth on Medusa. Who is telling the story and what is the POV? How does that influence the description of Medusa and the events? Highlight the text that helps you determine this.**

> Once a beautiful maiden with shiny, flowing locks of hair, Medusa dared to compare her beauty with that of Minerva. As punishment, the goddess of wisdom changed Medusa's gorgeous ringlets into hissing serpents. Medusa became a monster so frightfully ugly that anyone who looked at her face instantly turned to stone. She lived in a cave, surrounded by the stony figures of animals and people who had had the misfortune to catch a glimpse of her.
>
> One night, while Medusa slept, Perseus entered the cave. He sneaked carefully inside, using a shiny shield as a mirror to avoid looking directly at Medusa. When he found her, he cut off her head and presented it to Minerva.

▶ **Now read excerpts from a different tale about Medusa:**

Medusa Tells All: Beauty Missing, Hair Hissing
by Rebecca Fjelland Davis

▶ **From the title, what can you infer about the point of view?**

> I am Medusa. You've seen my face before. It's supposed to be one of the scariest in the world. But let me tell you—it's *not* my fault I'm scary! It's all Athena's fault.
>
> Everybody *loves* Athena. She's got the biggest, most beautiful, most famous temple in the world dedicated to her: the Parthenon in the city of Athens.
>
> But Athena is a big BULLY!
>
> Want proof? Here's the real story.

▶ **Who is telling the story and what is the POV? How does that influence the description of Medusa and the events? Highlight the text that helps you determine this.**

> You wouldn't know it now, but I was born beautiful. *Stunningly* beautiful. Everybody wants to be beautiful. There's nothing more important than beauty.

▶ **How would you describe Medusa? How is this different from the classic myth?**

▶ **Medusa is punished by Athena for Poseidon's interest and then this happens . . .**

> Yes, at the time, I was horrified when my hair came to life. But I have to take a moment here to say I don't understand all the fuss. Who cares about a few little poisonous snakes anyway? They never bite anyone! Ever!

(Continued)

(Continued)

Ok, the truth is that nobody ever gets close enough to me for my snakes to bite. Everyone is too—shall we say—*petrified*.

Some time later a "hero" came to town. His name was Perseus. He was half-god and half-man. His job was to take something from me: MY HEAD. And who do you think was helping him? Athena, of course. She couldn't be satisfied that she made me into a monster. No, she wanted to finish me off.

Athena had given Perseus her shield. It was as shiny as a mirror so he could see me without looking directly at me. Stygian nymphs had loaned Perseus the cap of invisibility so I couldn't see him coming. And Hermes, the messenger god, had given Perseus winged sandals so he could fly to me without making a sound. Everyone was against me.

It wasn't fair!

▶ Write about reading: **Now that you've read both myths, answer this question: How does point of view affect the way events are described? Explain the events from both perspectives.**

Note: Rebecca Fjelland Davis delivers the "real story" of the famous serpent-haired figure in Greek mythology, and her conversational tone makes it an accessible, easy read. The first person point of view is peppered with modern diction (e.g., "Athena is a big bully!" and "It wasn't fair!"), which enhances the funny, flippant tone. Students often take on the attitude of, why do we have to learn about all these ancient goings-on? That's why satirical send-ups on mythical figures from ancient Greece are valuable bridge-builders between young readers and history.

Analyze Contrasting Points of View

BEST THE TEST

In Grade 5 and up, compare and contrast is a staple of testing. Give students plenty and varied practice with this skill, but keep it authentic and engaging by having students apply it to texts *they choose*. Other tips:

- Students constantly compare movies, sequels, sneaker brands, apps, musicians, restaurants—you name it. So harness the power of these real-life comparisons as the basis for oral and written opinions that pit one student's point of view against another's.

- As you read aloud various texts, invite students to notice moments when characters most display divergent takes on events

LESSON PREP

- Photocopy Two Views (page 130) and the excerpts from *Wonder* (page 131). Share the prompts from Lesson 19 (page 122).

- Read a full-length novel narrated by multiple characters so you know it well. You can plan to teach the entire novel or just have students work through the excerpts.

INTRODUCE IT

- Model how you consider different characters' points of view. Discuss with students that these characters are going to have distinct interpretations of and responses to the events.

- Using the excerpts from *Wonder*, talk through the distinct perspectives of four of the six characters who narrate the story.

To find out more about *Wonder* and R. J. Palacio:

- http://rjpalacio.com
- http://www.npr.org/2013/09/12/221005752/how-one-unkind-moment-gave-way-to-wonder

Because of Mr. Terupt by Rob Buyea

Books in a series to compare characters (e.g., Rick Riordan series, Harry Potter, Emily Windsnap)

An interview with R. J. Palacio: https://youtu.be/Hh5qbE62IyY

HOW TO USE THE GRAB AND GO PAGES

- **Option 1**: Hand out copies of the *Wonder* excerpts on page 131, and have students notice point of view in this story. These excerpts are from the beginning chapters and introduce a different character narrating the story. Each excerpt also focuses on the narrator's relationship with Auggie (the main character).

- Through student discussion, unpack the point of view.

- Hand out the Two Views template on page 130 and ask students to compare and contrast Auggie with another character in the novel.

- **Option 2**: Use these excerpts to help you work through a shared reading of the entire novel, stopping at the beginning of each new character/narrator's part to discuss what you notice.

- **Ongoing**: After working through an entire novel as a shared text, expect students to transfer these skills to their independent reading and writing.

- Have students use sticky notes to mark details in their independent reading that support their thinking about differing points of view and how these are developed. They can refer to the prompts/questions that help readers focus on point of view.

- Create a matrix like the Character Matrix at **http://resources.corwin.com/evidencebased writing-fiction** and hand it out to students when you want them to do deeper work on multiple characters' different perspectives.

MORE TEMPLATES TO SHARE WITH STUDENTS

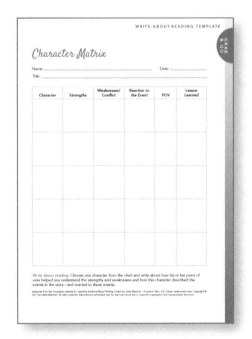

  Available for download at **http://resources.corwin.com/evidencebasedwriting-fiction**

Two Views

Name: _____   Date: _____

Title: _____

Directions:

Every character experiences minor and major events differently. Choose two main characters from the story you are reading, and reflect on how they think, feel, and act in either an important scene or the entire story.

	Character 1 would say:	Character 2 would say:
Setting		
My wants/conflicts/dreams . . .		
Other characters' agendas . . .		
The basic problem leading into the event . . .		
Possible resolution . . .		
Why I acted that way . . .		
What I learned . . .		

Explain how the narrator's point of view influences how the story and the events are described and explained.

Available for download at **http://resources.corwin.com/evidencebasedwriting-fiction**

EXCERPTS TO WRITE ABOUT

Wonder

by R. J. Palacio

Auggie *Ordinary* [p. 3]

I know I'm not an ordinary ten-year-old kid. I mean, sure, I do ordinary things. I eat ice cream. I ride my bike. I play ball. I have an Xbox. Stuff like that makes me ordinary. I guess. And I feel ordinary. Inside. But I know ordinary kids don't make other ordinary kids run away screaming in playgrounds. I know ordinary kids don't get stared at wherever they go.

If I found a magic lamp and I could have one wish I would wish that I had a normal face that no one ever noticed at all. I would wish that I could walk down the street without people seeing me and then doing that look-away thing. Here's what I think: the only reason I'm not ordinary is that no one else sees me that way.

. . .

My name is August, by the way. I won't describe what I look like. Whatever you're thinking, it's probably worse.

▶ **What is Auggie's POV? How does he describe himself? Highlight where in the text you find clues to how he views himself.**

Via *A Tour of the Galaxy* [pp. 82–83]

August is the Sun. Me and Mom and Dad are planets orbiting the Sun. The rest of our family and friends are asteroids and comets floating around the planets orbiting the Sun. The only celestial body that doesn't orbit August the Sun is Daisy the dog, and that's only because to her little doggy eyes, August's face doesn't look very different from any other human's face. To Daisy, all our faces look alike, as flat and pale as the moon.

I'm used to the way this universe works. I've never minded it because it's all I've ever known. I've always understood that August is special and has special needs. If I was playing too loudly and he was trying to take a nap, I knew I would have to go play somewhere else because he needed his rest after some procedure or other had left him weak and in pain. If I wanted Mom and Dad to watch me play soccer, I knew that nine out of ten times they'd miss it because they were busy shuttling August to speech therapy or physical therapy or a new specialist or a surgeon.

Mom and Dad would always say I was the most understanding little girl in the world.

. . .

So I've gotten used to not complaining, and I've gotten used to not bothering Mom and Dad with little stuff. I've gotten used to figuring things out on my own: how to put toys together, how to organize my life so I don't miss my friends' birthday parties, how to stay on top of my schoolwork so I never fall behind in class. I've never asked for help with my homework. Never needed reminding to finish a project or study for a test.

(Continued)

▶ **How does Via describe Auggie? What is her relationship with him? How does her POV differ from his?**

Summer *Weird Kids* [p. 119]

Some kids have actually come out and asked me why I hang out with "the freak" so much. These are kids that don't even know him well. If they knew him, they wouldn't call him that.

"Because he's a nice kid!" I always answer. "And don't call him that."

. . .

Who knew that my sitting with August Pullman at lunch would be such a big deal? People acted like it was the strangest thing in the world. It's weird how weird kids can be.

I sat with him that first day because I felt sorry for him. That's all. Here he was, this strange-looking kid in a brand-new school. No one was talking to him. Everyone was staring at him.

. . .

So I just went over and sat with him. Not a biggie. I wish people would stop trying to turn it into something major.

He's just a kid. The weirdest-looking kid I've ever seen, yes. But just a kid.

▶ **How does Summer describe Auggie? What is her relationship with him? How does her POV differ from the other characters?**

Jack *Carvel* [p. 136]

I remember seeing him for the first time in front of the Carvel on Amesfort Avenue when I was about five or six. Me and Veronica, my baby sitter, were sitting on the bench outside the store with Jamie, my baby brother, who was sitting in his stroller facing us. I guess I was busy eating my ice cream cone, because I didn't even notice the people who sat down next to us.

Then at one point I turned my head to suck the ice cream out of the bottom of my cone, and that's when I saw him: August. He was sitting right next to me. I know it wasn't cool, but I kind of went "Uhh!" when I saw him because I honestly got scared. I thought he was wearing a zombie mask or something. It was the kind of "uhh" you say when you're watching a scary movie and the bad guy like jumps out of the bushes. Anyway, I know it wasn't nice of me to do that, and though the kid didn't hear me, I know his sister did.

▶ **How does Jack describe Auggie? What is his relationship with him? How does finding out the POV of different characters help you understand Auggie? What do you still want to know? How would you describe Auggie?**

Note: In each of these excerpts, the author is describing story events from different characters' points of view. Interestingly, what unites them is that each character to a great extent *is influenced by what others think*. And what others think and say shapes their self-concept. Auggie is ready and willing to be normal, but people in the world around him avert their gaze, and don't treat him normally. Auggie's sister, Via, accepts her role as a planet orbiting the sun of her special needs brother. Her parents of necessity typecast her as the "most understanding little girl in the world," and so she has shaped her behavior to be independent and compliant, despite what she might "normally" want to think, feel, and do had she not had a brother with these health challenges. As your students read these excerpts and discuss point of view, have them look at it through this lens of how each of them is after the same thing—to fit in and belong.

SECTION 5

Visuals

Visual images draw us into books. Think of those big old novels by Dickens, Thackeray, and Eliot and how they lure even the most literary of us in with a four-color cover image. Think of the way visuals lead our youngest readers to "read" books by using the pictures to tell the story. Think of our English language learners and how viewing pictures can be the great equalizer. And lastly, think of the last time you read an article in some business or science journal that, well, befuddled you until your gaze landed on a bar graph or colorful chart that made it astoundingly easy to understand the concept.

Visual images are not just pretty window dressing on text. More and more, they are vital features of our information-soaked global world. They can add an aesthetic beauty to words, and they can impart razor-sharp, cool data to help us comprehend with their added benefit of color and shapes.

In the lessons that follow, you will see that I like to begin this quest for visual literacy by having students feel the *tone* and *mood* of pictures and how this enhances the tone and mood created by the words. I tell students that tone is the narrative voice in which the story is told. We can make this concept concrete for students by using different tones of voice: gentle, stern, angry, and so on. The tone then creates the mood for the piece. Some books maintain the same mood throughout (e.g., *In November* by Cynthia Rylant is calm throughout the book), while novels have multiple moods that reflect the action and the characters' changing states of mind.

Mood and *tone* are terms that can easily be embedded in daily instruction with books you share in class. The goal as usual is to get students to understand and apply these concepts of literature independently—to be metacognitive about them.

Lesson 21 includes a link to a PDF of a presentation by Molly Bang. It is an excellent set of slides to acquaint yourself with how to analyze visuals, and it can also be used with students. Don't be limited to just traditional books; bring in artwork for students to analyze, movie trailers, YouTube videos, graphic novels.

As students progress through the grades, they are asked to make connections between a text and a visual or oral presentation. They compare and contrast; analyze how elements contribute to meaning, tone, and beauty of a text; or analyze the effects and techniques unique to each medium. Think of how many times students read the book and then view the film, which then leads to a critique of which was better and why.

How does this fit with testing? Illustrations are often embedded in excerpts on texts, and students are asked what these add to the overall meaning. In addition, the more tests are online, the more students are exposed to watching videos and responding to them. There are also questions that compare and contrast a written piece to a short video clip.

Watch Leslie Teach!

Video 5: **Watch Leslie use picture books to teach students how to read visuals for clues on mood, setting, and plot.**

Go to **http://resources.corwin.com/evidencebasedwriting-fiction** to see the lessons and guided practice in action.

How Illustrations Add to Meaning/Mood

Mood: *It was a dark and stormy night. . . .* Mood is a literary element forged with a combination of descriptive words and a reader's knowledge of the characters' state in any given scene. It's the atmosphere in the text that evokes a certain emotion. Basically, it's the way a reader feels when reading a scene, chapter, story, or poem. Writers use diction, sentence style, setting, tone, and other devices to create mood.

PROMPTS FOR THINKING ABOUT HOW ILLUSTRATIONS ADD TO MEANING/MOOD

- How do the illustrations add to my understanding of the characters? The setting? The plot?

- How do the illustrations help to create mood?

- What do the illustrations in this book give me that the words don't?

- What do I notice about the illustrations and the technique? Color? Size? Placement? Shading?

- How would I describe the illustrations, and what do they reflect?

 Available for download at
http://resources.corwin.com/evidencebasedwriting-fiction

BEST THE TEST

Although only a handful of test questions depend on visuals, it's important to teach students how to look at illustrations through both an aesthetic and a critical lens. Here are some ways to do it:

- Teach students how to analyze photos and illustrations for mood, bias/point of view, characterization, and historical setting.

- As a class, over time, do a mix of work with visuals. Besides books, use technology to analyze movie trailers and videos and for students to record their thinking and responses.

- Look at an array of famous paintings throughout history, analyzing how color, style, perspective, and so on convey information, emotional import, and mood.

- Have students use smartphones, tablets, or other devices to take photos of important illustrations and then record their thinking either orally or in written form. Or take apart wordless books (laminate) and have students analyze the text. The bottom line: Always pay attention to how illustrations enhance understanding of the text.

LESSON PREP

- Make copies of Imagine the Story With Pictures (page 138) and the illustration on page 139.

- Familiarize yourself with techniques that create mood (see link below for a great slideshow to share and discuss with students).

- Choose a wordless picture book and familiarize yourself with the mood and how illustrations add to the mood. I use *The Flower Man* by Mark Ludy, which uses black and white and shades of grey (drab!) and then begins to slowly add color to show the positive changes happening. In addition, the color shows how the main character impacts others. Finally, this book has many mini-stories happening on its pages that students can repeatedly revisit.

- If possible, gather sets of wordless picture books. Another option is to scan them so students can access them on iPads, computers, or online.

- Gather Caldecott-winning books and have students analyze *why* these books received the award. For older students, find books that have been turned into movies. Find the scripts that match plays or movies so that students can analyze how the text transferred to the directing.

INTRODUCE IT

1. Distribute prompts to students and/or display them on the wall as an anchor chart.

2. Also create your own anchor chart with the prompts.

3. Create another chart to record thinking (setting, characters, plot, mood, techniques). Or provide students with charts to record their thinking as you work through a shared text.

4. Tell students the purpose of the lesson—to use the illustrations in the book to describe setting, character, plot, and mood and *how* the illustrations do this. Share the book once through so students can linger on the pictures. (This can also be done on a document camera depending on class size.)

5. Have students turn and talk—sharing what the story is about.

6. "Read" the book again, thinking aloud and recording the specifics from the illustrations that lead to understanding (e.g., Setting at first is gray and rundown. Characters look unhappy. The only color is on the old man's scarf [main character]. He buys the house and plants trees—his house is in color, everything else is black and white and dreary. When he gives a little girl a flower, the color starts to spread).

7. After finishing the book, ask: What did the author/illustrator do to tell the story? What was the mood at the beginning? Did it change? Why and how do you know?

8. Model how you go back through the book and mark three of the most important pages of illustrations and how they help to answer the questions.

9. **Write about reading:** Co-construct a short response retelling the story with an emphasis on setting, character, plot, and mood. Explain how the illustrations depict this.

10. Tell students they will be doing this same process you are now modeling, answering the question: How does the author/illustrator convey the elements of the story through visuals?

Access a list of Wordless Picture Books at **http://resources.corwin.com/evidencebasedwriting-fiction.**

Wordless Picture Books

Re-Zoom by Istvan Banyai
Zoom by Istvan Banyai
Journey by Aaron Becker
Quest by Aaron Becker
Return by Aaron Becker
The Only Child by Guojing
Wave by Suzy Lee
Rainstorm by Barbara Lehman
The Red Book by Barbara Lehman
The Farmer by Mark Ludy
Flower Man by Mark Ludy
The Lion and the Mouse by Jerry Pinkney
Chalk by Bill Thomson
Fossil by Bill Thomson
Imagine a Day by Sarah L. Thomson
Imagine a Night by Sarah L. Thomson
Imagine a Place by Sarah L. Thomson
Imagine a World by Sarah L. Thomson
Free Fall by David Wiesner
Tuesday by David Wiesner

Journey by Aaron Becker

Zoom and *Re-Zoom* by Istvan Banyai

The Only Child by Guojing

The Red Book by Barbara Lehman

The Lion and the Mouse by Jerry Pinkney

Free Fall by David Wiesner

Interview with David Weisner: https://youtu.be/ZuIsAIKiNgY

Interview with Rebecca Kai Dotlich: https://youtu.be/6E5aYOt4g6Q

This PDF presentation by Molly Bang is an excellent way to acquaint yourself and/or your students with how to analyze visuals: http://blogs.bgsu.edu/hljorda1100/files/2013/10/Molly_Bang_How_Pictures_Work1.pdf

More about David Wiesner:

- http://www.davidwiesner.com

- http://www.hmhbooks.com/wiesner

More on Rebecca Kai Dotlich: http://www.rebeccakaidotlich.com

HOW TO USE THE GRAB AND GO PAGES

- Hand out to students copies of Imagine the Story With Pictures on page 138 and the illustration on page 139.

- Either in small groups, with a partner, or independently, students study the two illustrations, which depict the start and the end of a story.

- Ask students to write the middle of the story using the picture clues. This can be done in a short burst—30 minutes—and it's a great way to develop students' writing stamina.

- **On another day**: Have students read a wordless picture book using the same process you just modeled. This could be with actual books, online, or with books that have been taken apart and laminated for students to rearrange, sequence, and analyze visuals.

- Students can fill out the Imagine the Story With Pictures template or write on sticky notes.

- From there, have students write a retelling of the story, including setting, character, plot, and mood. Have them explain how the illustrations depicted these elements.

- **Ongoing:** Mine the rest of *One Day/The End: Short, Very Short, Shorter-Than-Ever Stories* by Rebecca Kai Dotlich and illustrated by Fred Koehler. It's a powerful resource for teaching story reading and writing with words and pictures.

The Flower Man
by Mark Ludy

Purpose: How do illustrations help the reader with MOOD, SETTING & PLOT?

The Flower Man is a wordless picture book with lots of mini-stories happening besides the main one. The reader can re-read and look at each tiny house and character and find a story. The main story is about the flower man and how he changes a town. At first the illustrations are gray, black and white which shows how drab and sad the town is. The only color is the sky and the flower man to show he is bringing hope and happiness. Each page adds more color as his house. A little girl gets color as she gets a flower, and people notice. Color spreads as flowers spread. Everything gets clearer, people are happier ~ LIFE returns to town. The flower man's house is also in the front of each illustration, so you see it first. At the end the town is in bloom and the flower man leaves and goes to a new drab (black, white, gray) town to start over.

The Flower Man

MOOD - beginning - SAD, DEPRESSED (color - gray, black & white)
middle - happy, joyful (color!)
end - first town - happy!
new town - hopeful that it will repeat

color spreads, reader's eyes change

SETTING - Town changes from disrepair ÷ ramshackle to vibrant

color spreads from bottom to top of pictures

PLOT - The Flower Man changes the town through his flowers.

color of objects see intensity/proximity

GRAB & GO

Imagine the Story With Pictures

Name: _____ Date: _____

Title: _____

	Evidence—cite the page number or explain how the illustrations help you appreciate the story.
Setting	
Characters	
Plot	
Mood	

What *techniques* does the illustrator use to help you understand?

Write about reading: Write a short retelling of the story, using the illustrations and the evidence from your chart.

EXCERPT TO WRITE ABOUT

One Day, The End

by Rebecca Kai Dotlich

Source: From *One Day, The End* by Rebecca Kai Dotlich, illustrated by Fred Koehler. Copyright © 2015 by Rebecca Kai Dotlich and Fred Koehler. Published by Boyds Mills Press, Inc. Used by permission.

How Illustrations Contribute to Meaning

BEST THE TEST

The sophistication of illustrations increases as students progress through the grades. Visuals displayed on tests will reflect this, and students need to notice more subtle hints and cues to both literary elements as well as the mood and tone.

● Analyzing visuals should be a component of reading whenever students read or view texts with a visual component. Paying attention to both the words and the visuals creates stronger readers!

LESSON PREP

● Make photocopies of How Visual Elements Add to Meaning (page 143) and the excerpts from *The Promise* (page 144).

● Move from wordless picture books to picture books where illustrations enhance the meaning of the text. Polacco and Van Allsburg books are excellent for this, as these are both the author and illustrator of the book, which creates power between the text and art.

● For older students, move to graphic novels and chapter books that mix illustrations and text.

● Give students practice with asking questions about book covers, using illustrations as a guide.

● Have *The Promise* by Nicola Davies available, which will allow you to share the color illustrations, or photocopy the excerpts from it (page 144) and distribute to students.

INTRODUCE IT

1. Model how illustrations enhance understanding of the text and tone with a shared picture book like *The Promise*.

2. Or model using the text excerpts from *The Promise* on page 144 and have students *create* illustrations that match their understanding of the text.

3. Guide students through the illustrations and the text and how they enhance understanding, especially about meaning and tone.

Access a list of Wordless Picture Books at **http://resources.corwin.com/evidencebasedwriting-fiction.**

Wordless Picture Books

Re-Zoom by Istvan Banyai
Zoom by Istvan Banyai
Journey by Aaron Becker
Quest by Aaron Becker
Return by Aaron Becker
The Only Child by Guojing
Wave by Suzy Lee
Rainstorm by Barbara Lehman
The Red Book by Barbara Lehman
The Farmer by Mark Ludy
Flower Man by Mark Ludy
The Lion and the Mouse by Jerry Pinkney
Chalk by Bill Thomson
Fossil by Bill Thomson
Imagine a Day by Sarah L. Thomson
Imagine a Night by Sarah L. Thomson
Imagine a Place by Sarah L. Thomson
Imagine a World by Sarah L. Thomson
Free Fall by David Wiesner
Tuesday by David Wiesner

Any books by Patricia Polacco are excellent for this.

Any books by Chris Van Allsburg are also excellent, especially *The Stranger* (pay attention to the illustrations where the trees are orange and green and to the illustration where the Stranger blows on the leaf).

The Invention of Hugo Cabret and *Wonderstruck* by Brian Selznick

An interview with Brian Selznick: http://www.readingrockets.org/books/interviews/selznick

HOW TO USE THE GRAB AND GO PAGES

- Distribute to students copies of How Visual Elements Add to Meaning on page 143 and the excerpts from *The Promise* on page 144.

- Two options for using these reproducibles:

  ○ **Option 1:** Use as a teacher-guided lesson. Use these excerpts to help you work through a shared reading of the entire picture book, *stopping at these points in particular* to discuss how visuals contribute to meaning. The illustrations that match the text excerpts are on pages 8, 11, and 13 in *The Promise*. Have students use the How Visual Elements Add to Meaning template to notice and annotate both illustrations and text from *The Promise* by Nicola Davies. These specific pictures in the book display the use of color in illustrations to convey mood and tone and how the character changes. The first illustration (p. 8) is dark and without color and shows fighting. As the character changes and realizes her path, color is added to the illustrations. Unpack the significance of the illustrations through student discussion, whether small group or turn and talks. Finish with writing about the reading.

  ○ **Option 2:** Use these excerpts as a teacher-guided lesson. Instead of using the How Visual Elements Add to Meaning template, have students create illustrations to match each of the three excerpts. Stop at each juncture and allow students to sketch. Encourage students to use color (or lack of) in these sketches and discuss *what* in the text led them to draw and color the way they did.

- **Ongoing:** Augment this practice by providing access to books with strong images that are highly evocative, highly detailed, or both, and expect students to transfer these skills of attending to visuals to their independent reading and writing.

- Have students use sticky notes to mark specific details in illustrations. They can refer to the prompts listed above.

- Have students use the How Visual Elements Add to Meaning template to record their thinking and then write a response to the question: How do the visuals contribute to the overall meaning?

- Use the excerpts from *The Promise* on page 144 as the basis for creating your own excerpts page or for finding illustrations and text that help students understand how the two contribute to meaning.

How Visual Elements Add to Meaning

Name: _____ Date: _____

Title: _____

Visual or Multimedia is _____

Directions:

Fill in the chart below, citing scenes/specific text language in the left column. In the right column, jot about how the visual contributes to the power of each literary element.

Text	Visual or Multimedia
Tone or mood is created with these words:	Tone or mood is enhanced by:
Setting is described with these words:	Setting is enhanced by:
Character feelings/wishes are revealed by these words:	Character feelings/wishes are enhanced by:
Plot is shown by these words:	Plot is enhanced by:
Theme/meaning is communicated by these words:	Theme/meaning is enhanced by:

How do the visuals contribute to the overall meaning?

_____

_____

_____

_____

Available for download at **http://resources.corwin.com/evidencebasedwriting-fiction**

EXCERPTS TO WRITE ABOUT

The Promise

by Nicola Davies

▶ In this story, the main character lives in a city that was "mean and hard and ugly." The character was "mean and hard and ugly" and lived by stealing (p. 8 depicts this). What is happening? What does the illustrator do to show the tone or mood?

Now read this text and highlight where it matches the picture. Or, if you don't have the book, think about what visual image the words help you to imagine.

> And then, one night,
>
> I saw an old lady down a dark street.
>
> She was frail and alone, an easy victim.
>
> Her bag was fat and full,
>
> but when I tried to snatch it from her,
>
> she held on with the strength of heroes.
>
> To and fro we pulled that bag until at last she said,
>
> "If you promise to plant them, I'll let go."
>
> What did she mean? I didn't know or care.
>
> I just wanted the bag, so I said,
>
> "All right, I promise."
>
> She loosened her grip at once and smiled at me.

What is the tone of this? What is the mood? If you were to sketch an illustration for this section of text, what details would you include? What colors would you use to evoke mood or meaning, and why?

▶ After the main character runs off, she opens the bag. On page 11, the illustration shows the character doing this. What do you notice about this illustration? How is it different from the last?

Now read this text and highlight where it matches the picture. Or, if you don't have the book, think about what visual image it helps you envision.

> But when I opened it . . .
>
> the bag held only acorns.
>
> I stared at them,
>
> so green, so perfect,

(Continued)

(Continued)

> and so many,
>
> and I understood
>
> *the promise*
>
> I had made.
>
> I held a forest in my arms,
>
> and my heart was changed.

Have the tone and mood changed? Why? What words help you discern this turning point? If you were to sketch an illustration for this section of text, what would you include? How would it differ from your first illustration? What colors would you use and why?

▶ **On page 13, the character has changed, as has the artwork. What do you notice about this illustration? What has changed? What has the illustrator done to help you understand the character?**

Now read the text and highlight where the words match your thinking about the illustration or think about what visual image it creates for the reader.

> I forgot the food and money.
>
> And for the first time in my life, I felt lucky,
>
> rich beyond my wildest dreams.
>
> I slept with the acorns as my pillow,
>
> my head full of leafy visions.
>
> And in the morning, I began to keep
>
> *my promise.*

If you were to sketch an illustration for this section of text, what would you include? How would it differ from your first two illustrations? What colors would you use and why?

▶ **Write about reading: If you read these excerpts *and* the illustrations in *The Promise,* answer this question: What does the illustrator do with the illustrations to create tone and mood? Does the mood change? How does the illustrator show this?**

If you created your own illustrations to match the text, answer this question: How did you decide what to draw using the author's words? What did you do in your drawing to show mood and tone?

Note: Nicola Davies's spare, poetic language is beautifully matched with Laura Carlin's painterly illustrations. Grey, grim washes capture how the city in which the young girl lives is impoverished, driving her to steal from an old woman. Notice the way the words are set up almost like a poem, adding to the spare but intense meaning. Noticing the pairing of "old and alone," "frail and dark," and "fat and full"—adjectives that bring an ironic sense of balance to a desperate scene, in which the girl "snatches" the bag from the elderly woman. Then, after "to and fro" the sing-song pairings devolve into lines that are ordinary, banal ("What did she mean? All right, all right"), the diction of someone impatient to get her way and be gone, unenlightened. By contrast, later, when the girl sees the acorns—and sees the light—the author shifts the cadence to something energetic: "so green, so perfect, and so many." These excerpts show us the power of word choice and sentence structure to enhance meaning.

Compare Text to Staged Performance

PROMPTS FOR COMPARING TEXT TO STAGED PERFORMANCE

- How is reading a play, poem, or story similar to and different from the experience of listening to or watching a recorded or live performance of it?

- How does the medium or format in which you experience the text affect your understanding or experience of it?

- How does the written story differ from the performed/produced version?

- How do the different techniques in various media affect the meaning and experience of the story, drama, or poem?

- Where does the film depart from and adhere to the original (written) text—and to what effect?

 Available for download at
http://resources.corwin.com/evidencebasedwriting-fiction

Diverse Media: This includes print, pictures, illustrations, and electronic and new technology.

BEST THE TEST

Compare and contrast is tested in a wide range of ways starting at fourth grade, and then hitting heavily at fifth grade and beyond. Providing students with a variety of ways to compare and contrast allows flexibility and the transfer to any situation. Here are tips to get the book/film connection going:

- Embrace the idea that visuals are highly engaging and students enjoy watching videos or performances, and you can make the experience rigorous.

- While watching entire movies can cut into class time, viewing movies as homework can support efficient use of time and appropriate homework.

- Choose novels and books for book clubs or literature circles that have been adapted to movies.

LeSSON PRep

- Photocopy Compare/Contrast Text to Movie or Play (page 148).

- Choose a book that has been turned into a movie or play. Have the movie available, too. (I use *The Fantastic Flying Books of Mr. Morris Lessmore* by William Joyce and the 15-minute film version from 2011.)

INTRODUCE IT

1. Distribute prompts to students.

2. Also create your own anchor chart with the prompts.

3. Hand out copies of Compare/Contrast Text to Movie or Play.

4. Read aloud *The Fantastic Flying Books of Mr. Morris Lessmore* one time through for students to enjoy the story and the illustrations.

5. Read the story again, this time co-constructing meaning with students and having them record their thinking about the literary elements on Compare/Contrast Text to Movie or Play (page 148).

6. Show the movie version of the book. If the movie is short enough, view once just to enjoy, then watch it again and begin to record thinking on the template. Either stop periodically to discuss and jot OR view a third time and stop, jot, and discuss.

7. **Write about reading:** Using the information on the template, write a compare and contrast piece.

8. **Ongoing:** Use Compare/Contrast Text to Movie or Play with additional texts and movies.

For more on Lois Lowry:

- http://loislowry.com

- http://www.npr.org/2014/08/16/340170478/lois-lowry-says-the-giver-was-inspired-by-her-fathers-memory-loss

For more on Roald Dahl: https://www.roalddahl.com

Fairy tales—"Sleeping Beauty" and *Maleficent*, "Rapunzel" and *Tangled*

Paired books/films: *The Giver* by Lois Lowry, *The Lightning Thief* by Rick Riordan, *Because of Winn-Dixie* by Kate DiCamillo, *Charlie and the Chocolate Factory* by Roald Dahl, *Divergent* by Veronica Roth, *The Hunger Games* by Suzanne Collins

Interviews with Lois Lowry:

- http://www.readingrockets.org/books/interviews/lowry

- https://youtu.be/YYGGs2lxtjY

For more on Roald Dahl: https://www.youtube.com/user/officialroalddahl

HOW TO USE THE GRaB aND GO PaGES

- When comparing and contrasting text to performances, it is beneficial for students to hold their thinking. Distribute the Compare/Contrast Text to Movie or Play template on page 148 prior to reading, listening, or viewing.

- In small groups, with partners, or independently, students fill out the template, recording information about the text. Discuss thinking.

- Repeat this procedure after viewing a performance. Discuss thinking, especially around how the two formats are similar or different.

- **Write about reading:** Use the template to scaffold a compare/contrast piece.

- Adapt this template whenever your students are doing comparing and contrasting work.

Compare/Contrast Text to Movie or Play

Name: _____ Date: _____

Title: _____

Text Format: _____	Movie or Play
Setting	Setting
Character(s)	Character(s)
Point of View	Point of View
Conflict or Problem	Conflict or Problem
Dialogue	Dialogue
Important Events	Important Events
Resolution	Resolution
Tone/Mood	Tone/Mood

Other "Noticings"

Text	Movie or Drama
(e.g., character thoughts, etc.)	(e.g., music, scenery, etc.)

Similarities:	Differences:

Analyze Text to Drama

BEST THE TEST

Drama and scripts are referenced on tests, so practice and exposure to these formats in authentic ways will transfer.

- Analyzing the director's intentions and so forth requires higher-level thinking and making inferences.

- Students need to understand that when transferring a book to the screen, not everything can be included. They need to be able to articulate why. For instance, in books written in third person omniscient, the reader is able to see what all the characters are thinking and doing; often in scripts and film, the viewer can only see actions/hear words and must make inferences/interpretations.

- While this isn't generally on tests, it's a life skill and part of the standards. Also, when students begin to realize the importance of writing scripts to creating films, it makes writing authentic.

LESSON PREP

- Read a full-length novel or script that has been adapted to the stage or a movie version. (A basic book is *Charlotte's Web*, but Shakespeare is also an option!)

- Have the visual version available to view in class or as a homework assignment.

INTRODUCE IT

1. Read the novel or script, either as a shared text or assign for literature circles or book club. Keep track of literary elements (character, setting, plot, theme, etc.).

2. When finished, students summarize the book, including plot, theme, and character response to challenges (e.g., An example of *theme* with *Charlotte's Web*: friendship overcomes all adversity; or being humble can be the greatest strength) or create a classroom chart with plot and

theme (e.g., The plot is that Wilbur is to be butchered and how can his friends save him?).

3. Watch the visual presentation of the book. Some options are the 1973 Disney cartoon and the 2006 film with Dakota Fanning. If you have time to compare all versions, that makes this even more advanced.

4. If viewing the film in class, stop it at important points to discuss similarities and differences between the film and the book. When you finish, discuss these and *why* there are differences, focusing on author's purpose. Add to the template.

5. **Write about reading:** Have students write a compare and contrast response. To move this to the seventh- and eighth-grade levels, have students respond to *why* they think the director made the decisions he or she did in transferring the text version to the visual version.

For more on E. B. White:

- http://www.biography.com/people/eb-white-9529308

- http://www.scholastic.com/teachers/contributor/e-b-white

- http://www.npr.org/2011/07/05/137452030/how-e-b-white-spun-charlottes-web

A wealth of info on Shakespeare:

- http://absoluteshakespeare.com

- http://www.biography.com/people/william-shakespeare-9480323

Charlotte's Web by E. B. White

Theatre for Young Audiences edited by Coleman A. Jennings

Romeo and Juliet by William Shakespeare

Reader's theater books are excellent resources

Charlotte's Web

Romeo and Juliet

HOW TO USE THE GRAB AND GO PAGES

- Distribute to students copies of Analyze Text to Drama: Compare/Contrast Text to Movie or Play on page 151.

- When comparing and contrasting text to performances, it is beneficial for students to hold their thinking, especially when focusing on the director's purpose/intent. Distribute the template prior to reading, listening, or viewing.

- In small groups, with partners, or independently, students fill out the template, recording information about the text. Discuss thinking.

- Repeat this procedure after viewing a performance. Instruct students to pay close attention to additions or omissions in the movie and play and to analyze how these demonstrate the director's intentions.

- Discuss thinking—especially around how the two formats are similar or different—with a focus on author and director.

- **Write about reading:** Use the template to scaffold a compare/contrast piece.

- This template can be tweaked to use whenever comparing and contrasting in the classroom.

Analyze Text to Drama: Compare/Contrast Text to Movie or Play

Name: _____ Date: _____

Title: _____

Text Formats: _____	Movie or Play
Author's Purpose	Director's Purpose/Intentions
Setting	Setting
Characters	Characters
Point of View	Point of View
Conflict or Problem	Conflict or Problem
Dialogue	Dialogue
Important Events	Important Events
Resolution	Resolution
Tone/Mood	Tone/Mood

(Continued)

(Continued)

Purpose

Text	Movie or Play
How does the author's purpose influence how the text is written?	How does the director's purpose/intention influence how the movie or play is presented?

Similarities	Differences

SECTION 6

Words and Structure

Vocabulary gives us power. Knowing what words mean and using them allows us to communicate. Kids want power, so showing them how to be curious about words, to be word collectors and connoisseurs, helps them become better readers. We want our students to be conscious of the words they read—both the ones they know and those they don't—and we want them asking questions (Nagy, 1988). One of the greatest gifts we can give students is to simply explain what a word means when a student asks.

The lessons in this section reflect my belief that when it comes to developing students' vocabulary and interest in words, it's most effective to treat students as active readers and oft-published writers! That is, I encourage you to dig right into vocabulary and *expect* that students can articulate *how* they figured out the meaning of an unfamiliar word. Presume, assume—whatever word you wish—that your students love language as much as you do, and your enthusiasm will be infectious.

The lessons and collaborative work in this section also emphasize *using* new words in writing, because the more we practice and apply vocabulary, the more the words stick with us. We want to glue new words into our long-term memory, and there is no better way to do that than to use them in our own voice.

And yes, vocabulary is tested—a lot! On the most current tests, students are asked to choose a meaning for a word *in context*. Often the word/sentence is embedded in a passage, and then for the test question the sentence is repeated. Think about that—*in context.* So while we should be saturating our students with vocabulary, we must also teach how to use context clues. Because on current tests there is also the follow-up question: Which of these sentences helped you determine the meaning? Let's face it, we could do worksheet after worksheet with this focus, or we can have students read authentically, noticing words on their own, and using the context to help them decipher meaning.

In the pages ahead, you will also see plenty of ideas for teaching figurative language, because it's another often-tested skill. But we aren't going to flood kids with worksheets on it. Instead, let's give students examples of well-written texts where authors use figurative language to create imagery that moves students' emotions.

Where do craft and structure fit in? Mostly through students' writing. Go back and forth between noticing these elements in reading and helping students use these same structures in their own writing. The important thing to remember is, if you hit craft and structure too heavily in reading only, students quickly adopt a "whatever" attitude. Make it matter to them by showing them how it makes their writing stronger—and easier to organize.

Watch Leslie Teach!

Video 6: **Watch Leslie guide students to attend to vocabulary and word choice in a text.**

Go to **http://resources.corwin.com/evidencebasedwriting-fiction** to see the lessons and guided practice in action.

Determine the Meaning of Words and Phrases

Interpret: This is one of the most loaded lit terms, because to interpret is to receive and understand information through the filter of one's experiences, beliefs, and knowledge. Thus, one reader is going to interpret the meaning of a symbol, a passage, or an entire novel uniquely, *even if/when the reader is basing her judgment on a solid foundation of text evidence.* No one explains the process better than Louise Rosenblatt (1978) and her transactional theory of reading. To make the definition concrete for students, *to interpret* is best understood in slow motion, if you will—as a way a reader explains to himself, or another, his understanding of a piece or whole of a text; it's the act of putting an author's text into more accessible, familiar language.

Literal From Nonliteral Language: Literal language is factual and explicit; the reader does not need to infer to glean the meaning. Nonliteral language implies figurative language—often similes, metaphors, personification, and also abstract words.

PROMPTS FOR DETERMINING THE MEANING OF WORDS AND PHRASES

- Who is the audience for this text, and what is the author's purpose? How do the words used reflect this?

- Which words or phrases on this page seem most important?

- Which words or phrases help me understand the literal action?

- Which words or phrases get me to "read between the lines" and infer meaning?

- How can I use words I do know to figure out the meaning of words I don't know?

- What words or phrases tell me most about characters, actions, events, or the setting?

- Which words or phrases help me understand the meaning of this portion or the text as a whole?

- How does the author's choice of words affect the meaning and tone of the text?

 Available for download at
http://resources.corwin.com/evidencebasedwriting-fiction

BEST THE TEST

Determining the difference between literal (right there on the page) meanings and inferential meanings is a skill that is necessary for comprehension. Surprise, surprise, this skill is called upon a lot on standardized tests! Have students attend to the following:

- Use context to figure out unfamiliar words so they don't miss cues to infer important meaning as they read on their own.

- During read-alouds and any instructional reading experiences, make sure students don't gloss over words and figurative language that intimidates them; create a culture of curiosity, where readers are not afraid to say they're stumped.

- Students should also have a wide repertoire of other strategies for determining meaning of unfamiliar words.

LESSON PREP

- Choose a book with (figurative) language so that students can decide the literal versus the figurative meaning of the words/phrases. (In this lesson, I use *Twilight Comes Twice* by Ralph Fletcher.) Familiarize yourself with the figurative language, but choose two to three specific examples to work on with the students (e.g., pp. 11, 17, 18).

INTRODUCE IT

1. Distribute prompts to students and/or display them on the wall as an anchor chart.

2. Also create your own anchor chart with the prompts.

3. Create another anchor chart with "Literal vs. Nonliteral" as the heading.

4. Tell students that today the purpose will be to look at Ralph Fletcher's use of language and to notice the difference between literal and nonliteral (inferential) meanings and how literal versus nonliteral affects the meaning and tone of the piece as well as the reader's understanding.

5. Ask if they know what *twilight* means. Discuss. If students don't know the definition, instruct them to pay attention to the text to see if they get clues as to the meaning (context).

6. Read through the entire book once so students are immersed in the language and the narrative.

7. When you finish, ask about the organization— was there a problem? (no). What was the mood? (calm). Did you notice if Fletcher used any figurative language? (personification). If students did not know the meaning of *twilight* at the beginning, ask if they can define it now and explain *how* they figured it out.

8. Read the book again, but stop at the pages you marked. Add this line to the anchor chart: "Slowly dusk pours the syrup of darkness into the forest." Divide the chart into two columns under that sentence and label them Literal and Inferred. Discuss with students what that sentence would mean literally. Record answers (you might even sketch). Then discuss what the sentence means inferentially. Which meaning do you think Fletcher wants the reader to use? Why?

9. Continue reading, stop at page 17, and write "Dusk prepares for the great celebration of night. It sets the table carefully: Venus, a few stars, perhaps a crescent moon." This time have students create two columns in their reading journals and jot the literal and the inferential meanings of this. Turn and talk and then record student thinking on the anchor chart.

10. Repeat once more with this line: "With invisible arms dawn erases the stars from the blackboard of night."

11. **Write about reading:** Have students choose one of these examples and write a short response explaining what it does for them as a reader—how it helps them visualize or understand the text better.

12. Tell students that as they read they should pay attention to figurative language and decide if it should be read literally or inferentially.

More on Ralph Fletcher:

- http://ralphfletcher.com
- http://www.ralphfletcher.com/tips.html

More on Anne Ursu: http://anneursu.com

Review of *The Real Boy*: http://www.nytimes.com/2013/11/10/books/review/the-real-boy-by-anne-ursu.html?_r=0

Twilight Comes Twice by Ralph Fletcher

The Real Boy by Anne Ursu

A reading by Ralph Fletcher: https://youtu.be/xPLKR3dxfZw

HOW TO USE THE GRAB AND GO PAGES

- Distribute copies of Look at Language: Words and Phrases on page 158 and the excerpt from *The Real Boy* by Anne Ursu on page 159, along with highlighter pens.

- Instruct students to read the entire excerpt through once.

- Working in small groups or with partners, students read the excerpt a second time, highlight unknown words, and jot in the margin their thinking about the meaning and *why* they think that.

- Circulate, reminding students to notice which words are literal and nonliteral, and what the author might intend by using them.

- Have students discuss their work with peers; each student/group can choose three words to record on the Look at Language template.

- This lesson should be replicated often throughout the year.

MORE TEMPLATES TO SHARE WITH STUDENTS

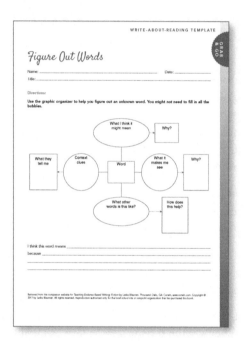

 Available for download at **http://resources.corwin.com/evidencebasedwriting-fiction**

Twilight Comes Twice
by Ralph Fletcher

"Slowly dusk pours the syrup of darkness into the forest."

LITERAL	FIGURATIVE (non literal)
· Dusk is holding a jar of syrup · The syrup is called darkness · Dusk tips the jar slowly and it pours into the forest. · That would be sticky!	When it turns from day to night, dusk comes first and it brings the dark slowly. Syrup is slow, so the dark comes down from the sky into the forests a little at a time instead of all at once.

"With invisible arms dawn erases the stars from the blackboard of night."

LITERAL	FIGURATIVE (non literal)
· You can't see dawn's arms · There are stars drawn on a blackboard with the word night on it. · Dawn has a chalk- board eraser. · Dawn erases all the stars.	The blackboard of night makes us see how black/dark it is with only stars on it. You can't see dawn (invisible arms) but as dawn comes the stars disappear first (erased)

GRAB & GO

Look at Language: Words and Phrases

Name: _____ Date: _____

Title: _____

Directions: **From your reading, choose three unfamiliar words and fill out the chart.**

Word:
I think this word means: The reason I think this is because: A word, phrase, or sentence from the text that helped me figure it out was:

Word:
I think this word means: The reason I think this is because: A word, phrase, or sentence from the text that helped me figure it out was:

Word:
I think this word means: The reason I think this is because: A word, phrase, or sentence from the text that helped me figure it out was:

Write about reading: Choose one of the words you "noticed" in your reading, and write it in a sentence:

_____

_____

EXCERPTS TO WRITE ABOUT

The Real Boy

by Anne Ursu

▶ Read through the entire excerpt once. Read a second time and highlight unfamiliar words. Annotate in the margins what you *think* the meaning is and *why*. You can draw arrows to words, phrases, or sentences that help you figure out the meaning.

▶ In this first paragraph of the book, notice how Anne Ursu describes the setting and the city of Asteri. Does she offer a contrast with words like *tangle, darkness,* and *shadowy*? What might she be setting up?

> The residents of the gleaming hilltop town of Asteri called their home, simply, the City. The residents of the Barrow—the tangle of forest and darkness that encircled the bottom of Asteri's hill like a shadowy moat—called Asteri the Shining City, and those who lived there the shining people. The Asterians didn't call themselves anything special, because when everyone else refers to you as the shining people, you really don't have to do it yourself.

▶ As you read on, notice how Ursu continues to describe the city of Asteri and the Barrow. What type of place is she describing? Good, bad? Or is it too early to tell? Notice the vocabulary here. Are there words you don't know?

> Massive stone walls towered around the City, almost as tall as the great trees in the forest. And, though you could not tell by looking at them, the walls writhed with enchantments.
>
> *For protection,* the people of the City said.
>
> *For show,* the magic smiths of the Barrow said. After all, it was in the dark of the Barrow where the real magic lay.
>
> And indeed, the people of Asteri streamed through the walls and down the tall hill to the shops of the Barrow marketplace, buying potions and salves, charms and wards, spells and pretty little enchanted things. They could not do any magic themselves, but they had magic smiths to do it for them. And really, wasn't that better anyway?

▶ In the passage above, Ursu is inviting us to infer that the residents of the gleaming city consider themselves superior to the magic smiths of the Barrow. The people of the Barrow in turn considered their surroundings better. She also reveals that each group needed the other. What details suggest this?

▶ Let's look at two more paragraphs, where the main character is introduced. How would you describe him? What words are you unsure of?

> The Barrow even had one magic worker so skilled he called himself a magician. Master Caleb was the first magician in a generation, and he helped the Asterians shine even more brightly. He had an apprentice, like most magic smiths. But like wizards of old, he also took on a hand—a young boy from the Children's Home—to do work too menial for a magician's apprentice.

(Continued)

(Continued)

The boy, who was called Oscar, spent most of his time underneath Caleb's shop, tucked in a small room in the cellar, grinding leaves into powders, extracting oils from plants, pouring tinctures into small vials—kept company by the quiet, the dark, the cocoon of a room, and a steady rotation of murmuring cats. It was a good fate for an orphan.

Note: The excerpts here are in the opening of a delicately written fantasy novel. Oscar is the hero of the story, who, like many a hero, is thrust out of his comfort zone by people and events around him. Notice the way the author introduces Oscar, and in just a few sentences describes his character fully. He is someone who is quiet and withdrawn, but also methodical and a good thinker, qualities that will serve him well as the plot unfolds.

Understand Figurative Language

PROMPTS FOR UNDERSTANDING FIGURATIVE LANGUAGE

- Which words or phrases are figurative language?

- Why is the author using them here?

- What types of figurative language are used?

- How can I use the surrounding sentences to help me determine the meaning of the figurative language (especially simile and metaphor)?

 Available for download at
http://resources.corwin.com/evidencebasedwriting-fiction

Figurative Meanings: Figures of speech (or figurative language) are those often colorful ways we develop of saying something; they include euphemism, hyperbole, irony, understatement, metaphor, simile, personification, and paradox, among others. Some of them are specific to an era, region, or social group and thus can confuse readers.

BEST THE TEST

Teach one type of figurative language at a time. I can't emphasize this enough, because students get confused when simile and metaphor are taught together. Provide several days' worth of models and practice before moving to another. Keeping anchor charts with definitions and examples from shared texts is beneficial. Revisit them often.

- Figurative language is a standard question topic on tests. A line will be cited and students must identify what it is. The follow-up question pertains to either what it means or why the author used it.

- Honestly, the best test prep is for students to be writing figurative language in their own pieces. It awakens an appetite for figurative language in the books they read.

- As students read independently, encourage them to notice examples of figurative language and share it on class anchor charts.

- Once students are familiar with many types of figurative language, have them highlight and identify as many as they can in excerpted texts for practice.

LESSON PREP

- Decide which type of figurative language you want to teach, and choose a book rich with examples (a list is available for download at **http://resources.corwin.com/evidencebasedwriting-fiction**) OR if students are familiar with all types of figurative language, choose a book with numerous examples; that is the focus of this lesson (in which I use *Hello, Harvest Moon* by Ralph Fletcher).

- Familiarize yourself with specific examples of figurative language in the text (e.g., alliteration: "double-dipped," "lonely lunar light"; simile: "Milkweed pods have cracked open, spilling out spores like tiny moonlings floating up to their mother," "sprinkling silver coins like a careless millionaire"; personification, which there is a lot of in this text: "Hello, harvest moon. With silent slippers it climbs the night stairs," "The harvest moon has its own work to do. It paints the wings of owls and nighthawks with a mixture of silver and shadow," "The harvest moon moves the earth's waters. Grabbing whole oceans with its arms").

INTRODUCE IT

1. Distribute prompts to students and/or display them on the wall as an anchor chart.

2. Also create your own anchor chart with the prompts.

3. Ask students to share types of figurative language they have studied. Tell them that the first time they listen to the story they should see how many different types of figurative language Ralph Fletcher uses.

4. Read the book through once so students can listen to the words.

5. Ask what types of figurative language they think Fletcher uses. Create a chart or boxes on the anchor chart and label with Personification, Simile, Alliteration (and any others students say).

6. Instruct students to create a similar chart in their reading logs, and as you read they should record examples in the appropriate places.

7. Read through the story again, giving time for students to record.

8. **Write about reading:** Students should choose one of their boxes or columns and write a short response explaining how it helps them visualize the text (they might even want to sketch as well).

For an extensive list of books to teach figurative language, check **http://resources.corwin.com/ evidencebasedwriting-fiction.**

Books With Figurative Language

Princess Prunella and the Purple Peanut by Margaret Atwood
Snowmen at Night by Caralyn Buehner
Snow Speaks by Nancy White Carlstrom
Double Trouble in Walla Walla by Andrew Clements
Bat Loves the Night by Nicola Davies
One Tiny Turtle by Nicola Davies
White Owl, Barn Owl by Nicola Davies
No Two Snowflakes by Sheree Fitch
Hello, Harvest Moon by Ralph Fletcher
Twilight Comes Twice by Ralph Fletcher
Blizzard by Carole Gerber
My Mama Had a Dancing Heart by Libba Moore Gray
Come On, Rain! by Karen Hesse
Amber on the Mountain by Tony Johnston
Desert Song by Tony Johnston
Crazy Like a Fox: A Simile Story by Loreen Leedy
Stubborn as a Mule and Other Silly Similes by Nancy Loewen
You're Toast and Other Metaphors We Adore by Nancy Loewen
The Moonflower by H. Peter and Jean Loewer
Like Butter on Pancakes by Jonathan London
Punished! by David Lubar
My Best Friend Is as Sharp as a Pencil by Hanoch Piven
My Dog Is as Smelly as Dirty Socks by Hanoch Piven
Rattletrap Car by Phyllis Root
In November by Cynthia Rylant
Here Comes the Year by Eileen Spinelli
Rise the Moon by Eileen Spinelli
Song for the Whooping Crane by Eileen Spinelli
Three Pebbles and a Song by Eileen Spinelli
My Big Dog by Janet Stevens
Hide and Seek Fog by Alvin Tresselt
Quick as a Cricket by Audrey Wood

More on Cynthia Rylant:

- http://www.cynthiarylant.com

- http://www.npr.org/2013/11/10/243546854/ how-cynthia-rylant-discovered-the-poetry-of- storytelling

More on Gary Paulsen: http://www.trelease-on -reading.com/paulsen.html

Hello, Harvest Moon
by Ralph Fletcher

Canoe Days by Gary Paulsen

In November by Cynthia Rylant

Owl Moon by Jane Yolen

Any books by Jonathan London are wonderful for figurative language.

Poetry is one of the best forms for teaching figurative language.

An interview with Jane Yolen: http://www.readingrockets.org/ books/interviews/yolen

Presentation on Cynthia Rylant (subscription required): https://jr.brainpop.com/readingand writing/authors/cynthiarylant/ preview.weml

An interview with Gary Paulsen: https://youtu.be/Q7ADtOjxmRs

HOW TO USE THE GRAB AND GO PAGES

- Distribute Figurative Language Collection on page 165 and Excerpt to Write About: Figurative Language on page 166 to each student.

- Decide whether you want to use these resources as a teacher-guided lesson or have students work in small groups, with partners, or independently.

- Work though each excerpt, highlight figurative language, and annotate. Build in opportunities for students to turn and talk. (Key: *In November*—simile

and personification combined: "Without their leaves, how lovely they are, spreading their arms like dancers," "Like butter on pancakes"; simile, onomatopoeia, personification; *Canoe Days*—simile and metaphor).

- Have students use Figurative Language Collection to record their thinking and then choose one and write about it.

- Have students use Figurative Language Collection to collect examples of different bits of figurative language to share with the class. These can also be added to excerpt sheets.

SAMPLE TO SHARE WITH STUDENTS

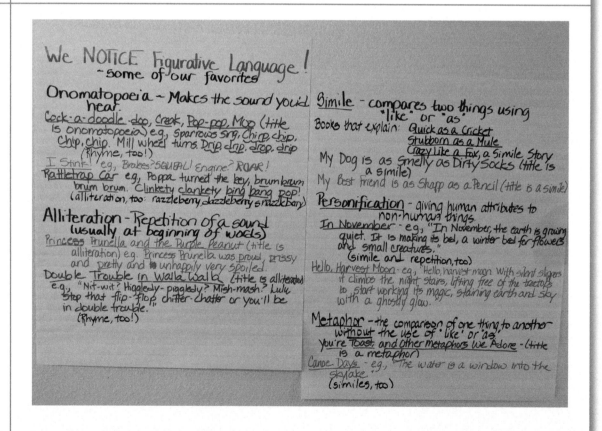

Figurative Language Collection

Directions:

See if you can find an example of each of these. Write down the line(s) and make sure you record the title! (*Rhythm and repetition aren't figurative language, but they make writing great!)

Alliteration	Assonance	Onomatopoeia
Title:	Title:	Title:
Simile	Metaphor	Personification
Title:	Title:	Title:
Hyperbole	Idioms	*Repetition and Rhythm
Title:	Title:	Title:

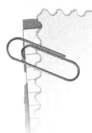

GRAB & GO

EXCERPTS TO WRITE ABOUT

Figurative Language

▶ Read these excerpts. Highlight the figurative language and then write in the margin what it is:

- onomatopoeia

- simile

- metaphor

- personification

▶ Next, write or sketch in the margin *why* you think the author used that. What does that do for you, the reader?

In November

by Cynthia Rylant

In November, the earth is growing quiet. It is making its bed, a winter bed for flowers and small creatures. The bed is white and silent, and much life can hide beneath its blankets.

In November, the trees are standing all sticks and bones. Without their leaves, how lovely they are, spreading their arms like dancers. They know it is time to be still.

Note: Cynthia Rylant is a writer known for her poetic prose. In these six sentences, she creates a powerful mood. I admire how she likens the earth to something that has will. The earth "is making a bed" for little flowers and creatures, like a loving parent does for a child. What else can you say about this first paragraph? Similarly, Rylant describes trees in a manner that makes us see them in a new way. How does she do that? Notice how she accomplishes a sense of peace, hush, and a rightness of nature. Which words most help her accomplish this mood?

Like Butter on Pancakes

by Jonathan London

Beyond the rim

of morning

the sun ticks

the birds talk

and the spoons sleep nestled

in the kitchen drawers.

First light melts

like butter on pancakes

spreads warm and yellow

across your pillow.

(Continued)

166 SECTION 6 ● **WORDS AND STRUCTURE**

(Continued)

A woodpecker pecks

On a lone pine

The sun ticks

The birds talk.

The rooster ka-ka-kadoos

on the henhouse roof.

A cloud drifts by

dragging a shadow.

Note: Jonathan London is also a musician besides being an author, and the rhythm of his words reflects this. There is a great deal of word play in this short excerpt. He plays with "tick talk," which kids will pick up on, and the image of time. He also meshes personification and similes to create imagery.

Canoe Days
by Gary Paulsen

One stroke of the paddle and we are gone, the canoe and me, moving silently.

Across water so quiet it becomes part of the sky, the canoe slides in green magic without a ripple,

Disappears like a ghost floating in the airwater over the playground where fish play.

The water is a window into the skylake.

. . .

But still now, everything frozen while the cold slash of a hunting northern pike moves like an arrow through the pads, looking, fiercely searching always for something to eat; and then he's gone into the green depths.

Note: Gary Paulsen is best known for the novel *Hatchet* and his strong depiction of character. Here he captures a simple slice of life—a descriptive picture book of what one might see from a canoe on a lake. Paulsen's use of figurative language creates visual and sensory images for the reader. He also uses metaphor beautifully.

▶ **Choose one of these excerpts and write a short response in which you address these questions: Why do you think the author chose to use figurative language in this way? How did it help you as a reader?**

Analyze Overall Structure

Analyze the Structure of Texts:
This refers to how authors organize their ideas and the text as a whole. Through structural patterns—at the sentence, paragraph, and whole-text levels—authors emphasize certain ideas and create such effects as tension, mystery, and humor.

PROMPTS FOR ANALYZING OVERALL STRUCTURE

● When I work to understand poetry, can I apply concepts like *stanza, rhyme, rhythm,* and *alliteration* to help me?

● When I read a play, how can I use my understanding of *casts of characters, settings, dialogue,* and *stage directions* to help me comprehend each scene?

● When I read prose, how can I use my understanding of *introduction, flow of paragraphs, conclusions, word choice,* and *voice* to enhance my understanding?

● Can I explain how poetry is different from drama or from prose using these terms? Can I explain how drama is different from the others?

● How do chapters develop the story?

● In drama, how do the scenes build on one another? How are they sequenced?

● In poetry, what is the main idea and how are the stanzas developed and sequenced?

 Available for download at
http://resources.corwin.com/evidencebasedwriting-fiction

BEST THE TEST

Knowing the structural elements, their definitions, and their usage is important, as students are tested on these. Stanzas, scenes, and paragraphs are all used on exams. More tips:

● Test questions might be phrased "In which stanza is . . ." and students need to know what a stanza is. This is true of dialogue, stage directions, and other elements.

● When students understand text structure and the elements, they can apply them to their own writing—another example of the reciprocity between reading and writing.

● Try to expose students to all three structures on the same topic at least once during the year.

LESSON PREP

- Choose a topic where you can find an example of poetry, drama, and stories. In this lesson I use fairy tales as they are short and accessible. Any fairy tale book will work for the story. *Mirror, Mirror* by Marilyn Singer is a wonderful book of poetry to use and any fairy tale reader's theater is short and can be incorporated into lessons. Familiarize yourself with the elements in each.

INTRODUCE IT

1. Distribute prompts to students and/or display them on the wall as an anchor chart.

2. Also create your own anchor chart with the prompts.

3. Tell students that you will be reading three different texts, all on the same topic (this may take multiple class periods), and you will be marking which elements are in the text.

4. Start with the fairy tale and read through, stopping at the elements and checking them off on the chart (sentences, paragraphs, dialogue, characters, etc.).

5. When you finish reading the story, discuss how these elements work together to make a story "prose."

6. Repeat the process with poetry.

7. Repeat the process with one script.

8. **Write about reading:** Co-construct a response about how readers can tell the difference between the three types of text and how the structure helps them understand the meaning. Include author's purpose!

For ELLs and students who may need extra support, download Determine Text Structure at **http://resources.corwin.com/evidencebasedwriting-fiction.**

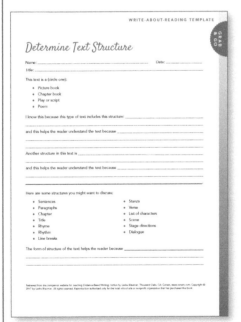

Mirror, Mirror by Marilyn Singer

Cinderella Outgrows the Glass Slipper and Other Zany Fractured Fairy Tale Plays by J. M. Wolf

12 Fabulously Funny Fairy Tale Plays by Justin McCory Martin

If you want to compare/contrast fairy tales to movies, any of the Disney fairy tales are wonderful. For shorter versions, YouTube has a plethora of animated fairy tales.

HOW TO USE THE GRAB AND GO PAGES

- Distribute to students copies of the Text Structure Analyzer on page 171 and excerpts from *No Two Snowflakes* on page 173.

- Guide students to read the excerpts and, using the Analyzer, determine whether it is prose, poetry, or drama.

- Allow students to discuss as they work—it deepens their understanding to share ideas.

- Next have students write a response explaining what type of text it is and why. Remind them to cite evidence from the text.

- A heads up: The excerpt is from the picture book *No Two Snowflakes* by Sheree Fitch. However, it is description, and in many parts it's written in poetic form. Ultimately, students should decide that it is almost a combination of prose and poetry. I really like using this particular work, because it awakens students to the reality that what they read often blends aspects of several forms/genres.

- If possible, read the entire book with students so they have an understanding of the overall structure.

- Use Text Structure Analyzer often throughout the year.

MORE TEMPLATES TO SHARE WITH STUDENTS

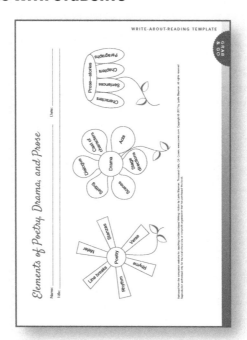

 Available for download at **http://resources.corwin.com/evidencebasedwriting-fiction**

Text Structure Analyzer

Name: _____ Date: _____

Title: _____

Directions:

- Look at the elements of text. Write a short definition or give an example of each.

- As you read prose (stories), poetry, and drama, place an X in the appropriate box.

Element	Stories (Prose)	Poetry	Drama
Chapters			
Characters			
Dialogue			
Line breaks			
Meter			
Paragraphs			
Plot			
Rhythm			

(Continued)

(Continued)

Element	Stories (Prose)	Poetry	Drama
Scenes			
Sections			
Sentences			
Setting			
Stage directions			
Stanzas			
Theme			
Verse			

Choose one of the types of text and write a response explaining *how* the elements you checked help structure or organize the text and how that helps the reader understand the meaning.

_____

_____

_____

_____

_____

_____

_____

_____

EXCERPTS TO WRITE ABOUT

No Two Snowflakes

by Sheree Fitch

▶ Use your Text Structure Analyzer checklist and what you know about poetry, prose, and drama to figure out how this piece is organized. Highlight and annotate your thinking.

1.

Dear Araba,

You asked me to tell

you about snow. Well, there are many

kinds of snow . . .

Some mornings the sky is grey and close

to the earth

all flannel and still, as if the day were

holding its breath.

▶ **From this first excerpt, what type of text do you think this is? Why?**

2.

Some days, snow is splinter sharp

needlepoints in skin

sounds like small stones

thrown at windows.

Turn your back to the wind, come in

by the fire with me.

We'll sip hot chocolate, eat cinnamon toast

tell stories till we nod asleep

to the snapcrackle music of wood

burning

the sifting sound

of snow drifting

against glass.

▶ **Now what are you thinking? Why?**

(Continued)

(Continued)

3.

Snow   sometimes sugar frosting

Snow   sometimes windwhipped waves of white

Snow   sometimes designs you find in dunes of sand

Snow   sometimes the trace of bird feet or a secret code left by rabbit paws.

The trees after snow?

Branches wearing long white gloves

    crystal chandeliers in a palace of glass

       stillness

         emptiness

▶ **That isn't the ending, but from these excerpts, how would you classify this? What is the structure?**

▶ **Task: Write a response explaining what type of text it is and why, citing evidence from the text. Why do you think the author decided to write it this way?**

Note: I encourage you to share the full picture book with your students. While it's free verse poetry, its storyline is that a Canadian boy writes to his pen pal, who lives in a tropical country, where snow never falls. Notice the way Sheree Fitch captures the diverse physical attributes of snow (it sifts, drifts, can feel like "needlepoints," hushes the sounds to a soft "flannel"). In addition, she beautifully conveys people's experience of it and the attendant rituals it brings, in sipping hot chocolate by the fire or gazing at its "windwhipped waves of white." Fitch, with illustrations by Janet Wilson, has created a book that students will be inspired to emulate.

Have your students study Fitch's techniques and try their hand at describing rain, or snow, or summer, or thunderstorms to a reader who has never experienced it.

Compare, Contrast, and Analyze Structure Between Texts

BEST THE TEST

Comparing and contrasting text structure is central to standardized tests. Students identify what elements are in each text and then discuss similarities and differences. Other tips:

- Tests usually focus on poetry and prose when comparing/contrasting.

- Give students practice with writing—present them with a text written in one structure and have them rewrite it using a different structure (prose to poetry, prose to drama, etc.).

LESSON PREP

- Collect two texts with different structures. Examples are Jacqueline Woodson's *Locomotion* (chapter book written in poetic form—novel in verse) and *Peace, Locomotion* (chapter book written like letters), or any Shakespeare stories and plays.

INTRODUCE IT

1. Use the Compare/Contrast Chart for Organization (page 177) for students to hold their thinking.

2. In small groups, with partners, or independently, students read both texts and record their thinking on the chart.

3. They then discuss their thinking with peers.

4. Using information from the chart, students write a compare/contrast piece or explain how the series of chapters, scenes, or stanzas fit together to provide the overall structure.

For ELLs and students who may need extra support, download Determine Text Structure at **http://resources .corwin.com/evidencebasedwriting-fiction.**

Winter Bees and Other Poems of the Cold by Joyce Sidman

Love That Dog by Sharon Creech combined with any books by Walter Dean Myers

Joyce Sidman reading her poetry: https://youtu.be/RfifKCtY-3s

An interview with Sharon Creech: https://youtu.be/9atmYRlEzCM

An interview with Walter Dean Myers: http://www. readingrockets.org/books/ interviews/myersw

WRITE-ABOUT-READING TEMPLATE

Determine Text Structure

Name: _____ Date: _____
Title: _____

This text is a (circle one):
- Picture book
- Chapter book
- Play or script
- Poem

I know this because this type of text includes this structure: _____
_____

and this helps the reader understand the text because _____
_____
_____

Another structure in this text is _____

and this helps the reader understand the text because _____
_____

Here are some structures you might want to discuss:
- Sentences
- Paragraphs
- Chapter
- Title
- Rhyme
- Rhythm
- Line breaks

- Stanza
- Verse
- List of characters
- Scene
- Stage directions
- Dialogue

The form of structure of the text helps the reader because _____
_____
_____

For more on Joyce Sidman: http://www.joycesidman.com

For more on Sharon Creech: http://www.sharoncreech.com

For more on Walter Dean Myers: http://walterdeanmyers.net/about

HOW TO USE THE GRAB AND GO PAGES

- Distribute to students the Compare/Contrast Chart for Organization on page 177.

- Use as a teacher-directed lesson, peer work, or independent work.

- Students read the poem first, annotating and recording their thinking. The purpose is to notice organization and how that helps understanding.

- Then students read the informational piece. While this is not prose, the organization is in paragraph form and it adds to understanding of the poem.

- Students record thinking on the write-about-reading template and then write a compare/contrast piece.

- These pieces can also be used to work on vocabulary with students.

Compare/Contrast Chart for Organization

Name: _____   Date: _____

Directions:

- Fill in the compare/contrast chart for your two texts.

- After filling in the chart, write a compare/contrast essay. How is the organization of both similar? How is the organization different? How does it help with reader understanding?

Similarities

Text: _____

| Elements |

Text: _____

| Elements |

| How organization helps with understanding |

| How organization helps with understanding |

EXCERPTS TO WRITE ABOUT

Winter Bees and Other Poems of the Cold

by Joyce Sidman and Rick Allen

▶ **Read the poem and notice the organization. Jot elements in the margins and think of how they fit together to provide the overall structure.**

The Whole World Is Melting

The whole world is melting!

The snow is slumping and dripping

and staining the bark black!

Roots poke from puddle,

and the leaf-litter where we live

is squishy-damp

     instead of frozen-hard,

and we have to move!

       We have to spring!

A mob of us, a mass of us, a throng of us

Launching ourselves to the top

Of the slippery snow,

     swarming its peaks and valleys!

And what will we find?

New moss, all ripe for slithering?

New loam, new love?

The whole world is melting

     and we are the first to see it,

wide awake on this lush winter day

as the trees grow wet and dark

and the earth warms and softens.

We are the first, first, first!

We spring!

    Spring!

      Spring!

(Continued)

(Continued)

▶ **What do you think this poem is about? How does the organization help you comprehend?**

Note: Notice how there is more than one speaker (*we*) and the author uses play on words (*spring*) to show both time of year and what the speakers are doing. However, without background knowledge the reader is hard-pressed to know what "creatures" are the speakers. The reader understands movement and motion—and the setting—but who or why? The word choice is wonderful for creating imagery and the setting. The companion piece unlocks the meaning and provides necessary background knowledge.

▶ **Now read the companion piece from the same author. How is this organized? How does it help with your comprehension?**

> On warm winter days when the sun is strong, tiny creatures called *springtails*—or "snow fleas"—swarm up through layers of snow to congregate on bare patches of ground or the snow itself. About the size of this "s," these sturdy, wingless creatures are neither true fleas (they don't bite) nor true insects (their bodies have fewer segments). They belong to a class of arthropods called Collembola, and are very abundant in moist places—up to 6,000 springtails in a square foot of soil!—feeding on leaf mold and fungi. There are many types of springtails, but those that emerge in winter have special antifreeze in their bodies that allows them to frolic in the snow, looking for new places to eat and reproduce. Although they cannot fly, they have an explosive way of moving: they fold a tail-like spike (called a furcula) toward their abdomen and lock it with a tiny hook. When they want to move, their abdominal muscles release the hook, which drives the spike downward and flips them up into the air. Unfortunately they can't control where they land, but a flip or two is usually enough to get them out of danger, or into new munching grounds.

▶ **How has your thinking changed? How did the organization of this text help your comprehension? After you read this piece, go back to the poem and reread. What do you notice? How has your understanding changed? Why?**

Source: "The Whole World Is Melting" from *Winter Bees and Other Poems of the Cold* by Joyce Sidman. Text copyright © 2014 by Joyce Sidman. Reprinted by permission of Houghton Mifflin Harcourt Publishing Company. All rights reserved.

REFERENCES

CHILDREN'S WORKS CITED

Bandyopadhyay, B. (n.d.). *The mighty.* Retrieved from http://www.pitara.com/fiction-for-kids/folktales/the-mighty

Bandyopadhyay, B. (n.d.). *The shepherd's mistake.* Retrieved from http://www.pitara.com/fiction-for-kids/folktales/the-shepherds-mistake

Cisneros, S. (2002). Eleven. In *Woman hollering creek and other stories.* New York, NY: Vintage.

Davies, N., & Carlin, L. (2014). *The promise.* Somerville, MA: Candlewick Press.

Davis, R. F., & Gilpin, S. (2014). *Medusa tells all: Beauty missing, hair hissing.* North Mankato, MN: Picture Window Books.

DiCamillo, K. (2001). *The tiger rising.* Cambridge, MA: Candlewick Press.

Firth, E. M. (1895). The mythical story of Arachne. In *Stories of old Greece.* Boston, MA: D. C. Heath.

Fitch, S., Wilson, J., & UNICEF. (2001). *No two snowflakes.* Victoria, BC, Canada: Orca.

Hall, D., & Moser, B. (1994). *I am the dog, I am the cat.* New York, NY: Dial Books for Young Readers.

Hughes, L., Rampersad, A., Hubbard, D., & Sanders, L. C. (2001). *The collected works of Langston Hughes.* Columbia: University of Missouri Press.

Hunt, L. M. (2015). *Fish in a tree.* New York, NY: Nancy Paulsen Books.

Jiménez, F. (1997). The circuit. In *The circuit: Stories from the life of a migrant child.* Albuquerque: University of New Mexico Press.

London, J., & Karas, G. B. (1995). *Like butter on pancakes.* New York, NY: Viking.

Lowry, L. (1989). *Number the stars.* Boston, MA: Houghton Mifflin.

Lowry, L. (1993). *The giver.* Boston, MA: Houghton Mifflin.

Lowry, L., & Ibatoulline, B. (2009). *Crow call.* New York: Scholastic Press.

Mr. Nobody. (1867). *Riverside Magazine for Young People.*

Palacio, R. J. (2014). *Wonder.* New York, NY: Random House.

Palacio, R. J. (2015). *Auggie and me: Three Wonder stories.* New York, NY: Alfred A. Knopf.

Paulsen, G., & Paulsen, R. W. (1999). *Canoe days.* New York, NY: Doubleday Books for Young Readers.

Phillips, H. (2012). *Here where the sunbeams are green.* New York, NY: Delacorte.

Rylant, C., & Kastner, J. (2008). *In November.* Orlando, FL: Voyager Books.

Sidman, J., & Allen, R. (2014). *Winter bees and other poems of the cold.* Boston, MA: Houghton Mifflin Harcourt.

Soto, G., Bachtell, T., Mostowy, M.-J., Clarke, K. C., & Poetry Center of Chicago. (2005). *Saturday at the canal.* Chicago: Poetry Center of Chicago.

Ursu, A. (2013). *The real boy.* New York, NY: Walden Pond Press.

Van Allsburg, C. (2008). My first step to the White House. In J. Scieszka (Ed.), *Guys write for guys read* (pp. 248–250). New York, NY: Viking.

Woodson, J. (2001). *The other side.* New York, NY: G. P. Putnam's Sons.

Zorn, S., Greenfield, G., & Bulfinch, T. (2003). *The classic treasury of Bulfinch's mythology.* Philadelphia, PA: Courage Books.

WORKS CITED

Atwell, N. (2007). *The reading zone: How to help kids become skilled, passionate, habitual, critical readers.* New York, NY: Scholastic.

Blauman, L. (2015). *The common core companion: Booster lessons, grades 3–5: elevating instruction day by day.* Thousand Oaks, CA: Corwin.

Fisher, D., Frey, N., & Hattie, J. (2016). *Visible learning for literacy, grades K–12: Implementing the practices that work best to accelerate student learning.* Thousand Oaks, CA: Corwin.

Harvey, S., & Goudvis, A. (2000). *Strategies that work: Teaching comprehension for understanding and engagement.* Portland, ME: Stenhouse.

Harvey, S., & Goudvis, A. (2007). *Strategies that work: Teaching comprehension for understanding and engagement* (2nd ed.). Portland, ME: Stenhouse.

Nagy, W. E. (1988). *Teaching vocabulary to improve reading comprehension.* Urbana, IL: National Council of Teachers of English.

Rosenblatt, L. (1978). *The reader, the text, the poem: The transactional theory of the literary work.* Carbondale: Southern Illinois University Press.

OTHER SUGGESTED CHILDREN'S BOOKS

Section 1. Evidence

Crenshaw by Katherine Applegate
The One and Only Ivan by Katherine Applegate
Cheyenne Again by Eve Bunting
Gleam and Glow by Eve Bunting
Walking to School by Eve Bunting
The Lotus Seed by Sherry Garland
The Music of Dolphins by Karen Hesse
Out of the Dust by Karen Hesse
"Jack Frost" by Anonymous (poem)
La Mariposa by Francisco Jimenez
The Giver by Lois Lowry (or any of the books
    in that series)
Crow Call by Lois Lowry
Number the Stars by Lois Lowry
Hatchet by Gary Paulsen
Back of the Bus by Aaron Reynolds
The Garden of Abdul Gasazi by Chris Van Allsburg
The Wreck of the Zephyr by Chris Van Allsburg
The Stranger by Chris Van Allsburg
Each Kindness by Jacqueline Woodson

Section 2. Relationships

Crenshaw Katherine Applegate
*Tom, Babette, and Simon: Three Tales of
    Transformation* by Avi
The Memory String by Eve Bunting
See the Ocean by Estelle Condra
Roald Dahl (any books)
Because of Winn-Dixie by Kate DiCamillo
The Tiger Rising by Kate DiCamillo
Flying Solo by Ralph Fletcher
Wilfred Gordon MacDonald Partridge by Mem Fox
Amber on the Mountain by Tony Johnston
Number the Stars by Lois Lowry
Mr. Peabody's Apples by Madonna
Esperanza Rising by Pam Munoz Ryan
Hatchet by Gary Paulsen
The Butterfly by Patricia Polacco

Pink and Say by Patricia Polacco
Thank you, Mr. Falker by Patricia Polacco
The Van Gogh Café by Cynthia Rylant
When I Was Young in the Mountains by Cynthia Rylant
Guys Read series Jon Scieszka
A Bad Case of Stripes by David Shannon
*Best Shorts: Favorite Short Stories for Sharing,
    Selected by Avi,* by Carolyn Shute
Liar and Spy by Rebecca Stead
Dad, Jackie and Me by Myron Uhlberg
The Tiger Rising by Kate DiCamillo

Section 3. Themes

The Crossover by Kwame Alexander
Reader's Theater Classic Poetry by Susan Brown
Gleam and Glow by Eve Bunting
The Memory String by Eve Bunting
One Green Apple by Eve Bunting
Smoky Night by Eve Bunting
So Far From the Sea by Eve Bunting
Train to Somewhere by Eve Bunting
Walking to School by Eve Bunting
The Wall by Eve Bunting
Coming Home, From the Life of Langston Hughes
    by Floyd Cooper
A Child's Anthology of Poetry
    edited by Elizabeth Hauge Sword
BookSpeak! Poems About Books by Laura Purdie Salas
Love That Dog and *Hate That Cat* by Sharon Creech
Locomotion and *Brown Girl Dreaming*
    by Jacqueline Woodson

Section 4. Point of View

Fractured fairy tales and the originals
Crenshaw by Katherine Applegate
The One and Only Ivan by Katherine Applegate
So Far From the Sea by Eve Bunting
Because of Mr. Terupt by Rob Buyea
Walk Two Moons by Sharon Creech
The Watsons Go to Birmingham
    by Christopher Paul Curtis
The Day the Crayons Came Home by Drew Daywalt

The Day the Crayons Quit by Drew Daywalt
What Mess? by Tom Lichtenheld
Baseball Saved Us by Ken Mochizuki
Heroes by Ken Mochizuki
Passage to Freedom by Ken Mochizuki
Wonder by R. J. Palacio
Pink and Say by Patricia Polacco
BookSpeak! Poems About Books
    by Laura Purdie Salas
How to Babysit a Grandma by Jean Reagan
How to Babysit a Grandpa by Jean Reagan
Memoirs of a Goldfish by Devin Scillian
Mirror, Mirror by Marilyn Singer
Dear Mrs. LaRue: Letters From Obedience School
    by Mark Teague
Detective LaRue: Letters From the Investigation
    by Mark Teague
LaRue Across America: Postcards From the Vacation
    by Mark Teague
LaRue for Mayor: Letters From the Campaign Trail
    by Mark Teague
Nettie's Trip South by Ann Turner
The Bracelet by Yoshiko Uchida
Encounter by Jane Yolen

Section 5. Visuals

Re-Zoom by Istvan Banyai
Zoom by Istvan Banyai
Journey by Aaron Becker
The Hunger Games by Suzanne Collins
Charlie and the Chocolate Factory by Roald Dahl
Because of Winn-Dixie by Kate DiCamillo

The Only Child by Guojing
Theatre for Young Audiences
    edited by Coleman A. Jennings
The Red Book by Barbara Lehman
The Flower Man by Mark Ludy
The Lion and the Mouse by Jerry Pinkney
Divergent by Veronica Roth
The Invention of Hugo Cabret by Brian Selznick
Wonderstruck by Brian Selznick
Romeo and Juliet by William Shakespeare
The Stranger by Chris Van Allsburg
Free Fall by David Wiesner
Charlotte's Web E. B. White
Fairy tales: "Sleeping Beauty" and *Maleficent*,
    "Rapunzel" and *Tangled*
Paired books/films: *The Giver* by Lois Lowry,
    The Lightning Thief by Rick Riordan

Section 6. Words and Structure

Hello, Harvest Moon by Ralph Fletcher
Twilight Comes Twice by Ralph Fletcher
Canoe Days by Gary Paulsen
12 Fabulously Funny Fairy Tale Plays
    by Justin McCory Martin
In November by Cynthia Rylant
Winter Bees and Other Poems of the Cold
    by Joyce Sidman and Rick Allen
Mirror, Mirror by Marilyn Singer
The Real Boy by Anne Ursu
Cinderella Outgrows the Glass Slipper and Other Zany
    Fractured Fairy Tale Plays by J. M. Wolf
Owl Moon by Jane Yolen

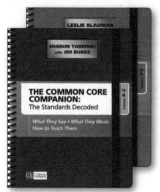

Bring Leslie Blauman to your school or district!

AUTHOR CONSULTING

Areas of Expertise

- Implementing the Literacy/ELA standards
- Reading and writing workshop
- Writing about reading
- Comprehension and thinking strategies
- Teaching research and nonfiction

Leslie can help you

- Use contemporary quality literature and nonfiction to teach students how to think deeply about texts and then to write in response to reading
- Develop your own engaging lessons based on key junctures in texts, incorporating best practices for discussion and written text response
- Understand the reciprocal process between reading and writing and the time-saving power of integration
- Explore ways to include quality mentor texts into the literacy block to boost student achievement in both reading and writing
- Evaluate student response and student writing to use for responsive teaching

About the Consultant

Leslie Blauman is one of the few author consultants who is still in the classroom. She has been teaching reading and literacy in the Colorado public schools for more than 30 years. Leslie's classroom is a working model for child and staff development in reading, writing, and critical thinking. While she works with teachers and students in a majority of the states and internationally as a consultant, her heart is in the classroom and she brings this to her writing and her consulting.

WHAT YOUR COLLEAGUES SAY

"As an International School in Japan, we were looking for a way to deepen our knowledge about best literacy practices. We were delighted when Leslie Blauman agreed to conduct regular video conferences with our teachers. After several conferences, teachers agreed that Leslie was very helpful and extremely knowledgeable—that it had been the best literacy professional development they have had. Teachers loved the way Leslie supported their learning by providing strategies and skills they could immediately implement. Thank you, Leslie!"

—**Paul Ketko**
Nagoya International School

"Great energy, LOVE the student examples and wonderful interaction (we actually got to do something!!!!)"

"Great ideas, good pace, and easy to implement."

"Enthusiasm and pacing—magnificent!"

"Energetic, fast-paced presentation. Great to hear from a practicing teacher. Realistic, hands-on activities to get kids thinking."

"Dynamic presenter! Amazing teacher with such energy. Lots of great ideas for content."

—**Comments from "Literocity" Conference**
Metropolitan School District of Pike Township

To bring Leslie Blauman to your school, call 800-831-6640

CL CORWIN LITERACY

CORWIN
A SAGE Publishing Company

N169H4

A SAGE Publishing Company

CORWIN HAS ONE MISSION: to enhance education through intentional professional learning.

We build long-term relationships with our authors, educators, clients, and associations who partner with us to develop and continuously improve the best evidence-based practices that establish and support lifelong learning.